What's Driving Your Business?

Steer Your Way to
Network Marketing Success

Luke Langsweirdt

What's Driving Your Business?

To connect with Luke and purchase copies of the book. Bulk Discounts for your team are available:
www.LukeLangsweirdt.com

Printed and bound in the USA

Table of Contents

Acknowledgements

Thank you to my beautiful and talented wife, Kortni. This book would not have been possible to write if she hadn't taken care of our wild two-year-old and newborn while I got to escape to the coffee shop and write. She is the most amazing, caring, thoughtful person I have ever met.

Thank you to my parents Lori and Larry Langsweirdt for always empowering me and feeding my creativity. I now realize after having two children what type of sacrifices you had to make to raise my sister Lana and me. I owe you more than words describe.

Lastly, thank you to the Harting family, Marcella, Jim, and Dallas for being true role models and elevating me personally and professionally. Your guidance and knowledge has allowed my family to live out our dreams and life the fullest.

Shout out to Nick Scavio, Matt Bogrand, and James Dillehay for your constant advice and my counsel to getting this book to print!

I appreciate the efforts of Jbfisherking for help on the cover and GrammarGal for assistance in the editing process.

Foreword

by Marcella Vonn Harting PhD

Life should not be a journey to the grave with the
intention of arriving in a pretty and well-preserved
body , but rather to skid in broadside in a cloud of
smoke, thoroughly used up, totally worn out, and
loudly proclaiming "Wow! What a Ride!"

Hunter S. Thompson

Picking up What's Driving Your Business is the first
step in taking yourself down roads you may never
have considered before and may not even have known
about. By the time you are halfway through reading it,
you will realize why you are where you are, and why
you have what you have at this point in your business.
You will have the answers that will help take you to
wherever you are capable of going. This book will help
you to choose your own path, and take charge of your
life and become the person you choose to be. You will
discover how to deal with circumstances and people
that may arise, no matter how difficult, overwhelming
or hopeless they may seem when they first appear.

We all admire those who seem to have the natural
ability to enter an unfamiliar social situation and begin
to engage others in conversation. These people have
learned necessary skills to become influential with everyone. This book is about the essential skills of identifying
people as vehicles driving you on the journey to achieve

extraordinary success with everyone. With this information we have the three fundamentals of human nature.

The first being the importance of feeling important. Second, people's primary interest is in themselves and third nature's law of equal returns. The more we know about people and ourselves the more value we can add and truly be of service. Which is the key to our success in all businesses. The reality is all is acquired skill of influential people, and like any other acquired skill, it can be learned, enhanced and perfected when you have the right information and the determination to learn. In a world of constant traffic jams, endless small talk, and overburdened schedules, Luke eloquently identifies our driving personality with vehicles, which we can all easily identify with!

So fasten your seatbelts. We're going on a thrilling journey. A journey on the road to your success and beyond by identifying and understanding practical guidance and powerful inspiration to readers searching for a proven framework in building a long-lasting legacy in network marketing. This book has given you the information you'll need to relate with others on a high level, to become a more interesting, influential, magnetic person and to help people reach their dreams, goals and desires.

Introduction

My legs were tired and my heart was still pounding. It was 2:00 a.m. on November 2, 2008. My business partner and I were hard at work. Our task? Removing all of the untethered assets from the restaurant we owned. On this dark night, we were facing the cold reality of our brick and mortar business—giant walk-in freezers, an industrial oven, and anything else not bolted down that would fit into the moving truck. Anything left behind would become the property of our landlord and be forever lost behind locked doors. Over the past four months, we gave it everything we had to stave off this fateful night. Six weeks earlier we laid off most of our employees. We had hoped the decreased payroll burden would keep the place afloat a little longer. It did, but not much longer.

A mere year earlier, it seemed like an honor to be one of the youngest franchisees of this particular restaurant chain. But I did not feel honored at that particular moment. By that night, I had sold all of my personal property with any value, liquidated my stock portfolio, defaulted on loans, maxed out my credit cards, borrowed money from friends and family, and stopped paying vendors. I had reached complete rock bottom. Drowning in debt, I was stressed and emotionally depressed. I am a failure. I am not business savvy. I took other people down with me. I am not enough. Bankruptcy is inevitable.

I was not the first casualty of the latest economic slowdown, and I would not be the last. As others did, I started to recover emotionally and financially. I switched my career path from restaurateur to accountant. Luckily, I excelled with numbers and percentages. I ended up working for diverse cross-section companies including a publicly traded restaurant chain, the world's largest golf management company, and a small but growing restaurant ownership group. By the end of my run, I had enough of wearing a tie to work every day and begging for a small raise each year as I inched up the ladder.

I know the struggles of a brick and mortar business and the challenges of the corporate world. After watching my own father work long corporate days my entire life, I knew that was not for me. My experiences have become my leverage to treat my network marketing business with respect and gratitude. Today my wife and I are full-time professional network marketers. In 2016 alone our sales reached well over seven million dollars. We have both reached the top 99.5 percent of business generators in our company, with over twelve thousand active members combined in our organizations. I was able to avoid bankruptcy and square up with my lenders. Our downlines have given us financial and time freedom beyond my wildest dreams. Do you know how good it feels to not have to ask a boss for time off? I get to be present for all of my children's magical moments. You too can have this freedom and take control of your own life's trajectory.

I have studied the network marketing industry, including many top leaders in this field. I have made personal growth a mission of mine and do my best to emulate great leaders. And I have attended countless three-day seminars to gain just a couple nuggets I could use for the rest of my networking career.

I have learned that network marketing is all about

relationships. Your time, efforts, and resources are extremely valuable as you grow your network. This book will teach you through a fun car analogy theme how to interact with certain personalities to maximize your team's growth. Find out who deserves your precious resources. These chapters will give you the keys to unlock successful interaction strategies, corrective actions for challenging personality traits, and vital components for building a long-lasting legacy with your network marketing team.

Now it is my turn to share my secrets with you. Don't be stuck sitting in traffic; now is the time to build your network and enjoy the financial and time freedom of the open roads.

CHAPTER I

Cruise Control

Cruise control is a unique feature on most vehicles. You can press a button and take your foot off the gas pedal and the car will continue going at your selected speed. Today, cars are even very close to driving all on their own while you just sit in the vehicle and enjoy the ride. Cruise control and self-driving cars remind me of one of the most enticing factors of network marketing, and that is, residual income.

Very few professions offer residual income. Marty Foley defines residual income (also called passive or recurring income) as "income that continues to be generated after the initial effort has been expended." Basically, money can be going into your bank account when you are on vacation or asleep for the night! With network marketing being about relationships, the more positive relationships you build, the more customers you gain, which leads to more residual income.

Professionals who earn residual income include actors, musicians, authors, network marketers, etc. Let's take for example Vin Diesel, who famously lives his life a quarter mile at a time. His role in the series The Fast and the Furious will most likely pay him every time a DVD is purchased or the movie airs on TV. Similarly, a musician can record a song and put the song up for sale on iTunes. When that song takes off and gets a million downloads, the musician gets a piece of the sales. Or an author can write a book and get paid from the sales as long as the readers purchase it.

The principal of residual income is to do all the effort upfront and have income flow in forever from those single efforts.

Now let's stretch our imagination and examine some jobs that get paid as active income (one payment for a specific task), and change our mind-set on what it would look like if the jobs paid out as residual income:

* A waiter takes a table serving newlyweds on a Saturday night and gives them great service. The waiter receives a tip at the end of the meal. With residual income, every time that couple eats at that restaurant again, the original waiter will receive a tip. Picture getting a tip month after month for one, two, ten years after waiting on those newlyweds! If a restaurant offered residual tipping for their staff, every waiter in the industry would jump through hoops to work at that restaurant, and give good service so the customers would come back!

* A real estate agent closes a sale and gets one commission on that sale. With residual income, picture this: after the sale, the realtor receives a small portion of the mortgage every month. With active income, when a realtor retires, their paycheck is zero. With residual income, they would still get checks long after they retired. Residual income can be a stress reliever and quality of life enhancer! (Trust me, coming up I will share a personal story of residual income from when my wife was pregnant.)

*I worked retail for a high-end jewelry store when I was younger and have the utmost respect for anyone in the retail industry. With December being the busy season, I remember extended hours and only taking a few days off around the holidays. I worked Christmas Eve for those last-second "oops, I haven't gotten her anything" gifts. Picture residual income for this career: I sell someone a watch and every time they wear that watch I get a small percentage each month. Imagine if you worked in the clothing department at a retail store and received a commission check every time someone wore a shirt you sold them. If you get enough small steady commissions coming in, they add up over time to a LARGE commission check.

Let's all channel our inner Vin Diesel and put our bank accounts on cruise control. To gain more residual income, connect with more people, and take care of your current customers.

Now that you understand more about residual income, let's look at a personal story of not quitting on the MLM profession even if you have crashed before.

CHAPTER 2

Crashed and Burned

If you have crashed and burned previously in network marketing or have a horrible taste in your mouth from another company, don't worry. It is not the end of your commute. Instead, it is just the beginning of your road trip. I am relieved I didn't let my horrible past experience dictate my future.

I joined my first network marketing company when I was twenty years old. It was a sunny eighty degrees out and not a cloud in the sky. I was walking my college campus at Arizona State, and I had a suit on because it was my fraternity's initiation week. A woman approached me and said, "You look like a business-minded person. I am giving a presentation at a local hotel and would love to have you as my guest because I think you would be perfect for this opportunity. You can make a ton of money, and it's a great service."

My immediate thought was, wow she has an eye for talent! I got the details for the presentation and ran off to class. Later that day, I ran into my buddy Scavio and invited him to go with me. We had no idea what to expect or what the opportunity even was. We had, however, recently watched the movie Boiler Room, where actor Ben Affleck has the famous line, "I drive a Ferrari 355 Cabriolet," and slides the keys across the table. So before going to the presentation, we made a pact that if they pulled any tricks like that we were standing up, tipping our hat, and walking out.

Later that day, we found ourselves sitting in a

Marriot boardroom with eight other clueless people. The presentation kicked off with two energetic females boasting about how they were going to change our lives tonight. They revealed to us the company was Excel Communications and that it was a network marketing company. The service sounded good at the time. To my recollection it was $55 for unlimited long distance calling for your home phone. You have to remember this was 2004 when everyone still had a land line and it was around 20¢ a minute for long distance.

The presentation continued and we start getting interested, when a tall skinny man walked into the room. He introduced himself, and within thirty seconds—you guessed it—the next thing out of his mouth was, "My red Ferrari is parked outside, and I paid cash for it," and his skinny little fingers slid the Ferrari keys to the middle of the table. Despite our pact, Scavio and I simply looked at each other with a slight chuckle and remained seated. An hour later we filled out the paperwork and put $400 on our credit cards. We were going to get rich with this revolutionary long-distance phone pricing. We could already smell the ocean breeze as we sat on the beach in Maui with residual income pouring in. I then proceeded to call everyone I knew to see if they would switch over to Excel with this red-hot deal we had! Out of fifty potential new customers only my uncle Bob saw the value in the deal. That or he was merely tossing his nephew a bone. Unfortunately, I received a call from Uncle Bob a month later. He said that he used to have automated voicemail and that it disappeared when he switched to my Excel. In an attempt to assist my best client, I called the company and was informed they didn't offer that. I called my uncle right back and said, "Bob, great news, I know what you are getting for Christmas . . . a brand-new answering machine!!" All in all I signed up one product user and two distributors (which included Scavio). Cell phones took over the world and the company ended up going bankrupt.

Looking back thirteen years later, I am very happy I didn't let that experience shape my future. My wife and I both have highly successful organizations, which has allowed our family to travel the world. My son had a passport at six months old and went with us on a company trip to Turkey, Venice, Croatia, and Greece. My daughter, who is now six months old, just received her passport to come with us on a company trip to Belize and Honduras. The residual income we are earning has allowed us to pay for our cars in cash, and the only debt we have is our mortgage of the dream home we purchased.

I also realize now that I failed in that business because I was not approaching enough people. I did not build a community of relationships. I went through my contact list and stopped there. I let a bunch of no's from my family and friends stop me. I also was not investing time, efforts, and resources into my one business builder who was excited. I did nothing for him; he must have felt like he was on an island.

I was just dipping my toes into network marketing with Excel Communications, and I've used my past as a reference and learning experience. Unlike with investing large sums into a brick-and-mortar business or taking out a loan for a start-up company, my consequences were minor. When Excel failed I did not lose my house or my car or have to file bankruptcy. It was simply, I am done promoting this company. Let me be very clear about one thing: I don't recommend you start changing companies all the time. What I advise you to do is find an MLM company you believe in, whose products and company align with who you are. If you are going to promote this company and brand yourself with it, it better be one you believe in.

Now that you have the insight to stick with network marketing, up next is one of my favorite personal stories of when an unplanned accident did not derail our income.

CHAPTER 3

Broken Bones and Booming Sales

One story I love, and that shows the power of network marketing, is about my wife Kortni, who has an amazing network marketing downline. She was pregnant with our first child, and broke her ankle multiple ways! We were told we were lucky the break happened in the second trimester because if it were the first or the third they would not have been able to repair the ankle for fear of the baby's health. They needed to do surgery and put in a nerve block around the knee to limit the baby from being affected from the anesthesia and surgery. This was a scary time for our family. I was worried about my wife and the baby. Medical bills were coming in, and after a metal plate and some screws, Kortni had a road to recovery. The month it happened, Kortni was unable to work her business. I can say with an open heart of gratitude that the month she was recovering was her largest volume in sales and the LARGEST commission check she had ever received up to that point! Let that sink in for a second . . . While pregnant and on bed rest she set all-time records for her business. Picture if she had had another profession. For most people, taking a month off would result in termination or no income. I can't say enough about the network marketing business model. It is priceless for the abundance and freedom it has given my family.

Now that you have a good handle on residual income and the benefits of relationship building, let's get into which people you should invest in. We are going to look at the different types of personalities and how to deal with them for your optimal success! To make it easier to understand I have created a car for each personality category. Learn which cars will take you to the top!

CHAPTER 4

Different Car Types

As you grow your network and interact with various personalities, you will notice some personality patterns. We are going to assume the personalities in this chapter are business builders in your team. I have created nine cars for the different personalities we most commonly see. In each car section, you will find a Vehicle History Report. Here is a summary of items you will see and how to look at this report:

*Mileage – The lower the mileage, the better the car. Higher mileage is a red flag.
*Mechanic Notes – This will give a brief description of the personality/car.
*Accident/Damage Report – This will give the thought patterns of this personality/car.
*Previous Owner – The lower the amount of previous owners, the better. Having a higher number of owners is a red flag.
* Warranty – The better the personality/car, the better warranty it will have. Some cars come with NO warranty, and that is a red flag.
*Above or Below Retail Value – This section lists what you should do with this car to optimize a successful interaction strategy.

The Vehicle History Report will be followed by a short story to bring this personality to life.

After explaining how to interact with this car to build a thriving organization, I dive into "Challenging Traits." Take a moment in this section to evaluate yourself. Think, do I ever exhibit a form of this trait? If a challenging trait resonates with you, hold back your tears. I've crafted the corrective action for each. Take a step back and look in the mirror in an honest way to improve yourself and enhance your relationships.

Cars to Leave in the Garage

Our time is one of the most precious things we have. In today's age, we have lost the value of our time. One of the biggest mistakes people make in their business is investing time with the wrong people. I have long heard the saying "work with the willing." Don't invest your time sitting in traffic (working with people who aren't going anywhere). In this section of the chapter you will discover why the Tow Truck, Convertible, and Roller Coaster are not vehicles that should take up your time, resources, and energy.

Vehicle History Report

Vehicle: CONVERTIBLE

Mileage:
112,000 miles

Mechanic Notes:
On a rainy day it is rare to be on the roads and see a convertible with the top down. Once the bad weather hits they are nowhere to be found. Everything needs to be going their way for them to succeed. When things get rocky they disappear. They are undependable and somewhat selfish. They will attend the fun events, but you won't see them hosting compensation plan meetings.

Accident/Damage Report Diagnostic:
*Some internal issues. Here are the poor thought patterns of this vehicle:
  • "The turnout for my class is lower than expected, so I am going to cancel the event."

•"That's too far to drive. I would go if it was in my backyard."
•"I need people to approach me for my product/service."

Previous Owners:
Nine

Warranty
Absolutely no warranty

Above or Below Retail Book Value:
The Convertible is well below average price. LEAVE THEM IN THE GARAGE! Don't invest your time trying to fix people. In this business, you can't wait around for good weather. It is not wise to dump your resources and time into a Convertible. There are others who deserve your time! Continue to invite them on group invitations, but don't stress out when they don't show up. When you do see them on the roads wave and smile.

Here's a story about Adam mentoring his protégée Nate, and realizing Nate is a convertible

Nate finally worked up enough courage to do an at-home class. He carefully thumbed through his Facebook contacts to invite his prospects to an educational class at his place that he would be co-hosting with his upline and sponsor, Adam. After scrolling and clicking he realized he had invited fifty-two people. He thought to himself, "Wow, I am not going to have enough room in my house." Adam assured him the rate of attendees is about 15 percent of those invited, so they would be lucky to have ten people arrive. As the date grew closer Nate noticed the RSVP rate was low, and only had four confirmed guests. Adam was excited to train Nate and work with some fun new people. He called Nate the night before to see what finger foods he could pick up on the way over for the class the next day. Nate's response shocked Adam: "Oh, the class, I canceled it. I felt like I would look like a nerd if only one or two people showed up. How awkward would that be!" Adam remembered his feelings on his first class and could sympathize with Nate, but explained, "Nate, I had two people show up to my first class, and one was my mom; the second person is now my top leader and makes over $6,000 per month. My willingness to look foolish and introduce my business plan changed their lives forever. It is not about having the perfect class; it is about being consistent with the classes." Adam realized Nate didn't understand, but thought he would be a superstar, so he continued to pour his efforts and time into Nate.

The upcoming months included Adam buying Nate a ticket to a big event in Orlando, Florida. Nate attended the event and looked to have finally turned the corner, ready to start taking this business seriously. Adam thought his investment had paid off, until he got a text from Nate: "Hey, bro, I'm going to be hella busy the next few months, will need to put the business on hold for a while. I'll give you a call in March." Adam still held out hope and kept buying tools and sending them to Nate, so when March hit he could hit it running. Nate actually read some of the books Adam sent, and started promoting the company on Facebook again. Nate was pretty excited he had a prospect that he almost closed. He explained, "So I posted this deluxe graphic and a friend hit me up, he asked to meet up and talk about the products. How cool is that?" Adam smiled and asked how the meeting went. Nate let him know, "I didn't meet up with him because the guy lived a 2 hours away. If he would have lived closer I would have been all over it!" Adam shook his head and now realized that Nate was not treating his business with any urgency or commitment. He knew it might be time to mentor a new rock star other than Nate.

Challenging Traits of Convertibles

1. They Don't Close

Remember, a convertible only comes out when the weather is good. They are great when after a presentation someone says, "I will sign up. Here is my credit card," but any resistance and they might say, "Okay, think about it and email me if you have any questions." A convertible gets nervous around closing and lets their belief of not being pushy/salesy get in the way of their success.

Corrective Action: *Make sure you get a yes or a no.* Ask the prospect right then and there if they would like to sign up right now. You need to get over being nervous about closing. Either the prospect says yes or no! What if they say yes and the products or business changes that person's life forever, simply because you had the confidence to ask them to sign up or join? You need to realize it won't be all sunny days. When things are not going your way and you get discouraged, change your mind-set back to positivity. Only you can control if you feel discouraged. Snap out of it and keep driving!

2. They Don't Do Their End-of-Month Checklist

The convertible somehow always gets too busy to do it, or it slips their mind until the month is almost over, and then they can't get a hold of anyone.

Corrective Action: You might have said, "I don't have a month-end checklist." MAKE ONE! What are the things you need to do the last seven days of the month? Examples include taking care of people whose auto-ships didn't process, reaching out to team members who are close to ranking up, giving recognition for those that did rank up, highlighting any promotions that are happening, and doing a monthly "care call." Go over your month-end checklist and have an accountability partner. Hold each other accountable to complete this each month.

3. They Have a Party Bus Mentality

A convertible likes good weather and the fun gathering. If there is going to be drinks and food there, a convertible is more likely to show up. If it is business training and self-development education you most likely won't see a convertible. They pick and choose what events will be a good time instead of what events give them the most value.

Corrective Action: If there is an event with even one of your downline attending, make every effort you can to be there. You are building a community, and your organization needs to see you actively participating on a consistent basis. Don't evaluate attending an event based on the enjoyment level; evaluate an event on what value can it provide to you. A compensation plan meeting may not sound sexy, but if you can get one small nugget out of it or connect with your team members and grow together, it can make a huge difference in your business.

LEAVE THEM IN THE GARAGE. Before we examine the next car, you might be thinking, "What does 'leave them in the garage mean'?" When leaving someone in the garage, it does NOT mean they are dead to you. It does not mean you should abandon them or be rude and nasty toward this person. It means you don't invest your time, money, or efforts into this person. There will be others that deserve that from you. Continue to invite convertibles to events and always be cordial. Make sure you don't burn any bridges by getting angry and letting loose with a derogatory text message. Just do not go out of your way to chase them down and try to change them. Let them know that when THEY decide to rev up their business you will be there to assist them. When someone is truly ready and the leverage is there for them to kick it into gear, you will see a change. They will be self-motivated and start taking action.

The next vehicle we will examine is the Tow Truck.

Vehicle: TOW TRUCK

Mileage:
132,000 miles

Mechanic Notes:
Would never show up unless you beg, push, harass them to attend! Very comfortable on their couch. Doesn't attend for themselves, shows up to please their upline. Loves to talk about quitting their current job, but currently lacks the fire to be self-starting in their network marketing business. Exemplifies laziness, non-motivation, and overall complacency.

Damage Report Diagnostic:
*Some internal issues. Here are the poor thought patterns of this vehicle:
- "You are going to have to pick me up and pay for my ticket."
- "Why hasn't my upline built my business for me?"
- "I am going to get rich, but I can't do two classes a month."

Previous Owners:
Eight

Warranty:
Absolutely no warranty

Above or Below Retail Book Value:
The Tow Truck is well below average price. LEAVE

THEM IN THE GARAGE. You don't have the time to tow people around. It takes too much effort and time out of you. You are going to the top of the mountain with or without them. It is too difficult to tow them up the mountain. There are other people and cars you need to align your business with to turn your efforts into a healthy growing business. Continue to invite Tow Trucks on group invites. Create a nice environment, in case the Tow Truck's leverage changes and they decide to leave the garage on their own.

Here is a story of a Tow Truck named Mike whose end fate is not how he pictured it:

Shane pulled into his driveway in his 1992 Honda Accord that somehow still ran with 213,000 miles on it. He had taught himself to maintain the vehicle for the last twenty years. He jumped out of the car, slammed the door shut, and jogged into the house with a big smile on his face. The past two years had been tough for Shane. His salary had been stuck at $55,000 because of a two-year salary freeze at his company. He would be turning thirty-seven a month from now and still drove the same Honda he got when he was sixteen. After getting married three years ago he was really starting to feel the pressure of finances and lack of success. If you would have told eighteen-year-old Shane that twenty years later he would be selling tires for the past decade while barely covering his mortgage and bills, he would have chuckled and thought that was a bad dream. Shane was voted most likely to succeed in high school and had big dreams of becoming a stock broker. His run of bad luck the last few years was compounded with a car accident that had some big medical bills attached. In

Shane's mind, this rough streak was all about to change as he barreled through the door to tell his wife of his new business venture.

A quiet coffee shop in West Seattle was the epicenter of Shane's new financial endeavor. He invited two guys, Mike and Ryan, who were hand-selected for a reason. Mike and Ryan arrived at the coffee shop at the same time and walked in to greet Shane, who was already at a table two espressos deep. Shane shook both of their hands and did not hesitate on why they were here, "So glad you guys took the time out of your day to have this meeting. I've got an opportunity to bring you in on that could change all three of our lives." Mike was open to hearing Shane out, as he had a little one on the way and was working ten-hour days as an account manager for a clothing line. Mike desired to be home more with his family. Ryan was a little more hesitant as to why he was invited to this meeting and came more out of curiosity.

Shane enlightened his future team on his grand idea. "Okay, I was approached by a network marketer whose company promotes legal representation. You educate people on why they need a safety net for legal purposes, and the customer can become a member by paying a small amount each month, like insurance. When you need any type of lawyer assistance they have a team of over a thousand lawyers who represent you for free. The legal representation covers the whole family and gives people the peace of mind that they always have a lawyer on call. The United States is the number one country in the world for lawsuits." Ryan cut off Shane right there, "That is all good, and it sounds like a great service they provide, but why did you invite Mike and I here? What does this have to do with us?" Shane gave a slight smile, as he was excited to explain the team he had already created in his head. "Network marketing is the ultimate team-building business. I thought long and hard with who I chose to partner with, and our collective skill sets are a match made in heaven for this business. I have been doing sales for fifteen years now and have mastered the art of suggestive selling, closing, and reading my customers. I am going to be the one putting on three presentations a week. Mike's been an account manager of over five hundred accounts for the last ten years. Once we close the client, Mike can take care of our customers just like he does now with his current job. Ryan, you may be our most valuable piece." Ryan has been a full-time freelance graphic designer. He takes a normal photo and can edit it into a work of art. His video creations are Spielberg-esque quality. Shane buttered up Ryan, "One key piece that will set our team apart is your graphics and videos. Our marketing will be impactful, eye-catching, and connect us with new customers. Ryan, your marketing will bring the people in, my presentations will close them, and Mike's relationship skills will be our recipe for success."

Unbeknownst to Shane or Ryan, Mike had been looking for another revenue stream and had actually tried another network marketing company three years ago. The problem was Mike would never do the follow-up and would skip most of the events. He was great at talking to people, but when he would get their contact info, it always just sat on his desk collecting dust. He loved the idea of being his own boss and having residual income pour in from a network marketing company, but he just didn't take the action needed to make it happen. The truth was, even at Mike's current job he was losing clients left and right by not taking care of their needs. He had over four hundred unanswered emails and twenty voicemails that had been there for well over six months. In Mike's mind he was going to jump at this opportunity to be able to support his growing family and be his own boss.

The coffee shop meeting lasted for three hours. Ryan needed to talk the option over with his girlfriend, because he was all in if he committed to this. Mike committed to Shane immediately and talked about how he couldn't wait to start. A week later the three were at the same coffee shop. After serious deliberation, Ryan was on board, with a slew of marketing ideas. All three gentlemen were excited and saw the vision Shane had laid out.

The first month went by, and the business was running like clockwork. The first presentation Shane put on had five guests, and three of them signed up to be legally protected for the future. As the months went by, Ryan and Shane noticed Mike had not been to the last four business meetings, with various excuses. They chalked it up to him being busy with his full-time job and pregnant wife. Ryan and Shane were naive and didn't realize Mike had done nothing to help the team over the last three months. Customers for their legal team couldn't get a hold of Mike, and the lack of effort began to surface to the team.

Mike began to complain that his network marketing checks were only $1,000 each month. Mike knew he couldn't support the family with this type of money. Oddly, Mike still didn't step up his game to drive business, take care of customers, or add anything of value to the team. He had developed a bad habit of playing video games, his vice being Madden 2017 Football for Xbox. Mike's indulgence in fast food fueled his weight gain, and he ballooned up well over 240 pounds, which is even scarier because of his five-foot-eight frame. Mike's wife, who was now seven months pregnant, scolded him, as he was putting a permanent indentation in the couch.

Ryan and Shane now realized that Mike's attitude toward the business had changed. For the past two months they had spent hours upon hours explaining to Mike and almost begging him to step up his game and attend the events. Shane realized that he was spending all his time trying to micromanage Mike, to no avail. Shane and Ryan decided it was in their best interest to not involve new customers with Mike. Mike's checks dwindled down to under $250 a month, and he had mentally checked out of the business. He still talked a big game that he desired to rise to the top, but it was all smoke and mirrors. After that month, Ryan and Shane did not hear from Mike for over five years.

Shane pulled his car into the coffee shop and while standing in line for his espresso noticed a familiar face taking orders. Mike saw Shane, and the embarrassment came over his face, as he now was a barista. They small talked a little, and Mike took a break to walk Shane out. Mike was surprised to see Shane walk up to a brand-new 2017 Jaguar XJL Sedan. Mike playfully said, "Well, Shane, looks like you upgraded that '92 Honda I remember you in." They both had a good laugh, and Shane responded with, "Yeah, business has been booming. I've got to run though; Ryan and I are taking our families to the Bahamas. Going to check out that shark water slide at Atlantis! Take care, big guy!" Shane drove off, leaving Mike in the parking lot of the coffee shop wearing a dirty apron.

Challenging Traits of Tow Trucks

1. Don't Show Up

A Tow Truck says they have every intention of going to their company's big convention. Yet when it gets closer, something comes up. I absolutely understand there are circumstances that won't allow going to conventions, but my mentor always tells her team you need to make every effort to get to our convention. This trait is not just for a convention but even local classes, group phone calls, training sessions, etc.

Corrective Action: There are going to be many times when you just feel like lying in bed or not booking the plane ticket. Please remember a saying and repeat it with me: "LEADERS SHOW UP." Say it again: "LEADERS SHOW UP." Keep this saying in mind when you are not in the mood to make the effort to be somewhere. Think about this, how can you expect members of your team to go to the convention if you can't make it there!

2. All Talk and No Action

This is the personality that says all the right things. "I am going to rank up and quit my job." "I am going to have financial and time freedom." "I would like to pay off my debt." Etc. Yet they do just that—talk. Talk is cheap and doesn't pay the bills! I do love voicing your intentions; however, there needs to be some action.

Corrective Action: Create a campaign and STICK to it. A campaign is having three dates on the books and at each event promoting the next event. If you are going to muster up the courage to do an at-home class, and it stops there, you may as well not even do it. If you are serious about building long-lasting residual income, you need to be consistent. A campaign with dates forces you to get off the couch and is much harder to back out of once you promote the event. At first you will most likely regret it before the event because of all the time and effort, but as soon as the event is over you will be happy and proud you stuck with it. You need to have a clear business plan on how you are going to back up all your talk. I suggest you write it down, brainstorm, outline, be specific, and put it into ACTION.

3. Not Following Up

Ready for the TRUE cliché? THE FORTUNE IS IN THE FOLLOW-UP. You would be surprised at how many customers fall through because the network marketer did not follow up! There are two types of follow-up people slack on:

> 1. When someone is interested in signing up and the communication stopped there. You were too busy, or felt uncomfortable reaching back out to them, or you thought too much time had passed, etc.
> 2. When you already have a customer or business builder and the communication stopped there.

Corrective Action: Track your prospects on an Excel spreadsheet or handwritten notebook. In Excel, highlight the prospects you still need to follow up with, in yellow. You focus more on the follow-up when they are highlighted yellow. You need to follow up with a customer after some time has passed and see how their experience has been, and if there is any way you can assist. A business builder is someone you should follow up with and see if there are any tools you can get in their hand. Don't forget you are there to serve them; help them get what they desire, and inevitably you will get what you desire. Another tip is when you have someone interested, don't just give them your card and cross your fingers hoping they will send you an email. A professional network marketer will see the interest and comfortably swap contact information with an invitation to meet up. Something like going to the dog park; meeting up for happy hour, a painting party at your house, or a BBQ to connect; taking the kids to the park; going to a sporting event or a boat ride; meeting up for coffee, etc. Finding a common interest and setting something up is so much more powerful than, "Here is my card, PLEASE email me." I am going to hammer this home: this is a relationship building business, and you need to have life experiences with your customers and business builders.

Vehicle: ROLLER COASTER

Mileage:
102,000

Mechanic Notes:
They are constantly up and down. One minute they are doing great and on top of the world, the next minute they are ready to quit the business. They see a vision of a lifestyle, but it can quickly get clouded by their own sabotage. The Roller Coaster is not emotionally stable—a true Jekyll and Hyde personality. The leadership from a Roller Coaster is difficult to follow due to the emotional swings.

Damage Report Diagnostic:
*Major internal issues. Here are the poor thought patterns of this vehicle:

- "I would do anything for financial freedom." Then one week later: "I think I am ready to quit because it is taking up too much time."
- "I am going to be rich; I just enrolled a new leader!" Then, "My new leader is not ordering anymore, time to cry for a week."
- "I love my current network marketing company." Then one week later, "I hate that old company. My new company is the best."

Previous Owners:
Ten

Warranty:
Absolutely no warranty.

Above or Below Retail Book Value:
The Roller Coaster is well below average price. LEAVE THEM IN THE GARAGE! Hopefully you can earn enough money to have a full-size roller coaster in your garage. It is not wise to pour your time, energy, and resources into a Roller Coaster. At any minute they could be gone. Continue to show your team what a constant, unwavering, confident leader looks like. You can't let them see you thinking about quitting. You need to be a stable role model that your team strives to become. YOU are their rock, YOU are their calming presence, YOU are the leader you need to be. You will see a Roller Coaster be completely engaged and then fall off the face of the earth. Do not take it personally; just assist the best you can when they are rolling, and let them go when they disappear. *One key piece of advice is to build a relationship with the Roller Coaster's downline, so when they do jump to another company you can step in and support their team members.

Here is a peek into the diary of a Roller Coaster

10/15/16

Dear Diary,

It's been over six months since my last entry. I'm writing because I am SOOO excited about my NEW network marketing company. This one aligns with EVERY-THING that is me. I LOVE makeup, and now I get to share it with everyone!! I signed up five people this week that I KNOW will be rock stars in my business. I assured them that if they have any issues I am all over it, assisting them the best I can. This makeup company uses only natural ingredients and is THE BEST on the market. I have an expo in a week that is going to be amazing. Life couldn't be better, and I am blessed to have finally found not only my calling, but also an avenue to financial freedom.

11/22/16

Dear Diary,

Why does everyone suck? My expo ended up costing me $500, and we only signed up one person. Total waste of time, I will NEVER do another one again. My five rock stars haven't ordered since I signed them up, and won't return my calls. I sent one of them a nasty note, and I don't even feel bad about it. I am sooo stressed out and don't even like this makeup anymore. I sent out an email to my organization to not contact me, and I am quitting. I hate dealing with these needy people calling me with every little issue. I'M DONE.

12/22/16

Dear Diary,

OMG, I just went to a holiday party and met the COOLEST person ever named Chris Jones. Chris sells greeting cards in a network marketing business. Who doesn't love getting cards in the mail? I told him how I hate my current job, and he is willing to work with me to quit my job. I think I manifested Chris into my life. This is finally my ticket. I've got a great feeling about this one.

01/18/17

Dear Diary,

Chris Jones can go to hell. He lied about his income, and I found out I am the only person he has ever signed up with his greeting card company. I didn't get rich in three weeks, and I'll never do another network marketing company again.

Challenging Traits of Roller Coasters

1. Keep Changing Companies

A Roller Coasters loyalty and commitment wavers constantly. They can be shouting at the mountain top how great their company is, and the next minute when there are issues or they see someone else successful in another company, they are ready to make the switch.

Corrective Action: Get with a company where others have made it and YOU feel it has a great product or service, buckle in, and RIDE IT OUT. If your enthusiasm for your product is fake, people will see through it and you will start thinking of changing companies. You lose some credibility when you are on your fourth network marketing company in two years. It is difficult to develop leaders and build trust with your customers. Your warm market becomes very cold when it is the third time you have approached someone with three different business plans or products.

2. They Start Off Hot Then Get Some Rejections Then Quit

They seem to be all in, then disappear. Completely hot and cold with their commitment.

Corrective Action: Quitting is not an option. If you need to vent privately, do it with your upline. When you're feeling discouraged, go to your upline. When you are feeling excellent, go to your downline. This business can be difficult, and most people at some point think about throwing in the towel, whether they host some events and no one shows, or their numbers are plummeting, the comp plan changes and cuts your check in half, people stop ordering, etc. You have to pick your head up, re-focus, and continue to build relationships. You need to work on your emotional state, get a physical activity you enjoy to let out some frustration, or do yoga and meditation to help calm and center yourself.

3. All Over the Place

They have a bunch of business ideas and have trouble finishing one. One minute they are building with expos and having some success, and the next minute they do a U-turn and exclusively build by mail outs. There is not much balance and consistency in their business game plan.

Corrective Action: Take your business growing ideas and make a list of them. Analyze the time it would take for each. Knock out the ones that do not take up too much time. After that, rank the ideas in order of which ones you feel are an effective income producing activity. Take action on the activities that will produce income. There are many times that someone will start building their business a certain way and have a little success, and then randomly stop that activity. Evaluate what works for you and stick with it for a consistent amount of time. Put intention and focus on the hours you have in the week to put into your business.

CARS TO TAKE HEAD ON

Buckle your seat belts, it is about to get bumpy. The Race Car and Lemon personalities are on the move. You need to take these vehicles head on and correct them before there is a crash. It may be awkward and uncomfortable, but it is for the betterment of your business and team members.

Vehicle History Report

Vehicle: Race Car

Mileage:
109,000 miles

Mechanic Notes:
A Race Car will win at all costs. They cross recruit and have unethical tendencies. They not only can ruin your organization, but on a grander scale they can get your entire company shut down. They cheat, lie, and steal their way to the top.

Damage Report Diagnostic:
*Some internal issues. Here are the poor thought patterns of this vehicle:
- "My goldfish loves the products. What do you mean they can't have a downline?"
- "Your upline is horrible. Switch to my organization. I will take you to the top!"
- "I can have you making $5,000 a month in six months, while only working two hours a week."

Previous Owners:
Six

Warranty:
Absolutely no warranty

Above or Below Retail Book Value:
The Race Car is well below average price. Confront the Race Car immediately. As a leader, you need to train them on how to do things the right way. If you let a Race Car continue their ways it will start affecting your whole team. It will be awkward and most people do not like confrontation, but know that your actions are to preserve you, your family, team members, and company. I typically do not come from a whistle-blower mentality. I try to deal with the person directly. If that does not change the unethical behavior, there are extreme cases where you need to contact the conduct department with your company. Do not let a Race Car take you and your company down.

Here is a story of a Race Car named Bernie, which is based on a true story regarding the FTC and the fate of Bernie's company

It is almost midnight, and the darkness of the apartment was pierced only by the glow of the computer screen. Operating this computer was Bernie, one of the up and coming network marketers in the industry. Bernie was growing his network marketing business fast and furiously. He was putting in the late-night hours because he had set a goal: to hit the next rank by Christmas time this year. This goal would push Bernie, as it was already in the hot months of July. This particular late night he was looking at all the events for professional network marketers in his area. Bernie manically believed if he could attend these events, he could steal plenty of network marketing business builders into his company. Yeah, sure, the event's planners said you couldn't talk about your company or try to recruit anyone, but in Bernie's calculating mind the rules didn't apply to him.

While at one of these events, he surprisingly saw Kelly. Kelly was a part of his current network marketing company. He politely invited her to sit next to him during this full-day event. While Kelly pulled out her laptop to log into their company's website, a light bulb went off in Bernie's head. He decided to sneak a peek at Kelly's password. He instantly had a flashback to high school, where he perfected his spy-like vision to look forward with his head while his eyes casually shifted down to the other students' answers.

Cheating to get ahead was nothing new to Bernie. Kelly calmly punched in her username and tabbed down to the password. Here was the moment of truth for Bernie. He actually got a rush out of times like this. As Kelly typed the password in, Bernie caught every letter: K-A-T-L-O-V-E-R. "Katlover, what a dumb password," he thought to himself. Not quite sure what he was going to do with this classified information yet, he jotted it down until he could brainstorm how to cash in on his knowledge.

Temperatures started to drop some and the leaves began to turn orange. Most people love this time of year, but Bernie was thinking how time was running out to rank up by Christmas time. His plan to recruit top leaders from other companies was not panning out. The few he did bring over left his organization within six months. It was turning into another late night. Bernie struggled to sleep while thinking about all the possibilities to bring in new recruits. His latest misleading idea was a minute-long video he put together showing his lifestyle as a network marketer. He showed off his Maserati (rented for the day), his two-story house boat (his uncle's friend's), and he even rented two kids to be in the video. Bernie directed them to pose as his own, because a family man is easier to trust. The cherry on top for this video was his income check of $35,000 for the month, which was forged in Photoshop. Surprisingly, the video received great attention on YouTube. The members started flowing in! Bernie was getting closer to his new rank, and his organization was growing. Sadly, his diabolical plans grew as well, and this time would cost him dearly.

Two weeks later, Bernie pulled out his notebook and saw a note from earlier in the year. Scribbled on a corner of his paper, it read "KATLOVER–Kelly." As soon as he read it a dark cloud came over Bernie's city and heavy rain started to pour. It was nights like this that Bernie's thoughts started racing around as he looked out the window and saw a full moon to partner with heavy lightning over his city. He opened up a web browser and logged into Kelly's organization with the stolen password. He discovered that her organization had over five hundred people. He now had access to all of the members' personal information. All Bernie could think of now was calling all of Kelly's people that were ordering large orders, and seeing if he could offer the world in hopes that they would switch to his team. After a hundred phone calls to his new "warm leads," Bernie was shocked to see how easily people could be bought. Some desired cash to switch, some just needed to hear Bernie would build their organizations for them. In total twelve people switched over! Bernie called them his "Dirty Dozen," and he trained them on his sneaky techniques. One technique which Bernie liked to call "college eats your cash" was pushed onto his Dirty Dozen. He unleashed his crew on twelve college campuses across the US to hold business meetings titled "You Don't Need College, Stop Wasting Your Parents' Money." The thought behind his meetings were to prey on young people and show them they didn't need a college degree. The scary part of this is how successful Bernie and the Dirty Dozen were.

Bernie's business soared, and now he really was making $35,000 a month. The bad part for Bernie is that with the growth it raised some red flags and the Federal Trade Commission started investigating the entire company's recruiting methods. The FTC soon found that Bernie's company was rewarding members for recruiting and not for selling product, coupled with the detailed strategy of targeting college students to quit college to become rich. The investigation ended with an FTC raid on the company's corporate office and all its assets frozen. The company was shut down overnight. Thousands of people who depended on the income from this company lost their businesses overnight. I wish this was just a fiction story, but is based on a true story.

Bernie, for whatever reason, did not even flinch. A week after the implosion of his business he was putting in another late-night lurking on Google to find the fastest-growing network marketing company to join. Let's just hope he doesn't burn his next company to the ground like the last one.

Bonus Story:
Here is another true story on why taking unethical

shortcuts can have serious downfalls. June 19, 1949, Bill France, the founder of Nascar held the first ever, strictly stock car race, for an even playing field. Glen Dunaway won the race, but they discovered he had modified rear springs, and he was awarded last place. Don't be Glenn Dunaway. Be Jim Roper, the guy who did things right and was awarded first place for his second-place finish in the first Nascar event.

Challenging Traits of Race Cars

1. Lying About Income and Efforts

A Race Car has a pattern of saying what people desire to hear. They mislead people by taking the one example of someone rising in the ranks and making huge money in a short amount of time with little effort. Those examples actually do exist, but this is not a fair representation of the averages. Network marketing is not a get-rich-quick scheme, and the Race Car does not fairly represent the foundation you need to build before consistent residual income arrives.

Corrective Action: Make a point to ALWAYS show your company's Income Disclosure Statement. My company has an excellent IDS. It gives the shortest, average, and longest amount of time it takes or has taken to hit each rank, as well as the low, average, and high monthly income for each rank. Use it as a tool to set realistic expectations for a new business builder. It will be extremely more effective if a business builder realizes they are embarking on a three-year journey to build a foundation and can mentally prepare for the long haul if they choose, versus the irreversible damage you cause when you mislead a new prospect by telling them they can retire in six months working one hour a week. What happens after the six months? You guessed it, they quit because it did not meet expectations.

2. Cross Recruit

Network marketing can be competitive. The Race Car likes to play in the gray area and has no regard for ethics. Cross recruiting is an industry standard word and is a Race Car characteristic. Cross recruiting means recruiting people already in your company, but not in your downline. Race Cars give promises and false hope that the grass is greener on their team. This is a quick way to build a toxic team and lose credibility within the company. My company has a policy that I could lose my whole organization for cross recruiting. It is NOT worth it.

Corrective Action: According to Worldometers there are 7.5 billion people on this planet with over 350,000 people born every day. Build within your organization; there are enough prospects for everyone. Cheer on other lines that are doing great. Don't compromise your reputation over cross recruiting. The way to build a team that is going to keep building and lasting is by doing it the right way. Also, people duplicate their experience. If I was a new hot shot that got cross recruited and offered $500 to switch teams, how do you think my mind-set will be to build? I will do what I know and start offering other rising stars $500 to jump ship and come on my team. It is a dangerous revolving door. Build by adding value to people's lives. Just because you are not cross recruiting, it does not mean you can't communicate with others that are not in your downline. I have excellent relationships with cross line members in my company. I constantly use them as a tool for resources, and they do the same for me.

2. Cheat and Manipulate

What are the loopholes? How can I get an unfair advantage? If there is a contest run, a Race Car will cheat their way to the top. They will look at the compensation plan and figure out how to exploit it unfairly for income or rank by doing things such as signing up dead people or faking a social security number, and my favorite is signing up their cat for auto-ship!

Corrective Action: Read the rules of the contest and obey them. You need to set an example of how to run your business with ethics and honor. If you have an idea and it is in the gray area, call the company and get approval. Realize that how you act is how your team will act. Build your organization the right way and sleep well at night!

Vehicle: Lemon

Mileage:
149,000 miles

Mechanic Notes:
The Lemon is always in the shop. They are always negative and drain your energy, time, and resources. They stir the pot and are constantly surrounded and looking for drama. It is the type of team member that you could fully support, but no matter what you do it will never be enough in their eyes. The Lemon is usually difficult to be around for long periods, and the glass is always half/empty.

Damage Report Diagnostic:
*Many internal issues. Here are the poor thought patterns of this vehicle.
- "I heard that leader bought their entire organization."
- "Our corporate executive team are a bunch of morons."
- "Let me post on Facebook everything that annoys me about my products and company."

Previous Owners:
Eleven

Warranty:
Absolutely no warranty

Above or Below Retail Book Value:
The Lemon is well below average price. Handle the Lemon immediately. Let them know that's not how you do things. We don't spread rumors. We choose great positive energy. If the compensation plan changed, they'll need to quit complaining about it, and get OVER IT. Address and sympathize with the Lemon's complaints, and find a solution with them if possible. I understand that every once in a while they just need to vent and let it all out. In that case just listen. It is key to understand the difference between occasional frustration and venting from constant year-round "Lemon" personality.

Here is an email from a Lemon to their upline

Dear Luke,

I hope this email finds you well. With you being my upline I chose to reach out and get your thoughts on some items. I have been building my business for five years now, but I am quite frustrated. Six months ago the company changed the packaging for some of our products. It is horrible! I do not deal with change very well and frankly took three months off from building to regroup. I sent out an email to my entire downline letting them know I hate the packaging and asked if they agree. As you can guess, I was not alone. Another setback for me was when the company changed the compensation plan two years ago. I was floored! My check went down $50 per month. Naturally, I took to a Facebook post to voice my frustrations on how GREEDY my company is. The world needed to know. I relied on that money. My company does not care about us little people.
Another issue I wish to ask you about is a problem

I am having with one of my leaders. Her name is Linda and she is always asking me to do stuff for her. I don't have time for three-way calls and brainstorming sessions. Can't she just figure it out? She is very annoying. To be honest with you, she needs to lose some weight. She is very fat. I am surprised her husband is still with her; he probably has someone on the side.

I heard that our company is being bought out. Is this true? I hate the current ownership and think they are incompetent. I would welcome this move, so I started a petition with my organization to push for them to sell. I do not know why they would sell, but anyone would be better. I am not sure the outcome of this petition but I have two hundred signatures and chose to raise awareness that we needed change! What are your thoughts? Let's do a call as soon as you can to discuss.

Cold Regards,
The Lemon

Challenging Traits of Lemons

1. Negativity Can Spread

Constant negativity can poison a team. Energy is contagious, whether it is positive or negative. Negative energy is draining to be around; it can take the wind out of someone's sails. And if you've ever been around one, you know a Lemon can and will complain about anything and everything!

Corrective Action: When something is upsetting you, you are probably not alone. Use your critical eye to identify the problem, find a solution, and then share it with your team. For example, if a Lemon was going to the convention and the local hotel was very expensive, a typical Lemon would just complain about how expensive it is. I suggest you acknowledge the steep price and brainstorm a solution. Maybe find a hotel fifteen minutes away for half the price and take a shuttle to the event, or see if there is someone willing to split a room. Even take action to the degree of organizing a "convention garage sale" to raise money for yourself or your team. A Lemon can be powerful if they use their own issues and turn them into solutions for their team.

2. Wastes Time on Things They Can't Control

A Lemon will harp on situations that they have nothing to do with or they can't do anything about. For example, if a company changes the compensation plan, they will complain about it until the moon comes back.

Corrective Action: Change your mind-set. Start using conscious language and feeding off of positivity. Worry about the things you can control. YOU can control your mood, your attitude, your brainstorm sessions for issues, etc. Acknowledge the comp plan change is a challenge, and then study it and share with your team the best way to capitalize on the new plan.

3. Creates and Attracts Drama

Whether it is with their customers, business builders, or new prospects, a Lemon has a history of stirring something negative up. They escalate situations that could have been diffused. A lemon spreads rumors and fuels gossip.

Corrective Action: Mind your business and stay with positivity as your driving force. Don't focus on someone else's marriage status, income, success. You need to take care of yourself and be a safe haven for people to contact, and not a pot stirrer. Give a gift to someone, show recognition to your team. It feels better! Wake up in the morning and show gratitude for what you do have.

CARS TO ASPIRE TO BE AND TO CULTIVATE

It's time to drop it into fifth gear. Identifying and knowing how to work with Ice Cream Trucks, Electric Cars, Ambulances, and Bulldozers is how you propel your growth into high speed. Start with yourself: emulate and become these leadership vehicles to build a long lasting-organization.

Vehicle History Report

Vehicle: Ice Cream Truck

Mileage:
9,200 miles

Mechanic Notes:
We LOVE Ice Cream Trucks. They play their music and drive through your neighborhood while people literally jump out of their house with money in hand!! They attract great people into their life and are true networkers. Ice cream trucks are usually involved in plenty of social networks, such as chambers of commerce, Rotary Clubs, happy hours with co-workers, softball leagues, weddings, and baby showers, and they seem to have a connection everywhere. Ice Cream Trucks are the type of people who sit on a plane and always have a conversation with the person next to them. By the end of the flight, they have the person's contact information and now have a new prospect. To an Ice Cream Truck, anyone is a potential customer.

Damage Report Diagnostic:
*No internal issues. Here are the positive thought pat-

terns of this vehicle:

- "I think my landscaper would love our products. I can't wait to have a conversation with him on Friday."
- "I love talking to people. It is fascinating connecting with a new person."
- "I don't judge a book by its cover."

Previous Owners:
Two

Warranty:
Has four years left or 100,000 miles of full bumper-to-bumper warranty.

Above or Below Retail Book Value:
The Ice Cream Truck is in excellent condition and is worth much more than the book value. Give them the keys. They are doing the number one thing that needs to be done to get your business to the top: talking to NEW people about their product or business opportunity. Make sure the Ice Cream Truck has a call to action to bring all the people they talk to. If your Ice Cream Truck team member lives locally and you host a monthly class, make sure they know all the details so they can make connections and bring new people to the class. For example, I host a monthly online event on Facebook. When I get the date on the books, I create a promo video for the event and make sure to send it to my Ice Cream Trucks and other top leaders to promote and invite. This is where third-party edification becomes powerful. The Ice Cream Truck does not have to be the expert—just the networker connecting people to the expert. If you come across a dynamite handout

or educational material, purchase some extra and send them to your Ice Cream Trucks. Stay in constant communication with these team members. Pour your time and resources into them and their downline by giving them extra attention with webinars, classes, events, pamphlets, samples, etc.

Here is a story of Marcy, who is a true Ice Cream Truck

The sun started to rise and light began to fill the master bedroom of Marcy's condo. She took the morning to relax and wait for the TV repairman to check out her satellite dish and why it was not spitting out her favorite programs! (If you are over seventy years young, you call TV shows "programs.") After the repairman arrived Marcy chatted him up a little bit and realized this man may need her products in his life but *he didn't know it yet.* She gave him the lowdown on her company and why it's the greatest and gave him her card!

She then drove down to her favorite lunch spot. Parking was rough so she decided to spring the couple bucks for valet. She saw the hostess, who directed her to a window view of the street—Marcy LOVES to people watch. Her favorite game is trying to guess people's occupation by looking at them. Since Marcy was dining alone that day, the waitress hung around a little and talked to her. Marcy then realized this young waitress would really enjoy her company's products, so Marcy filled her in on the latest and greatest products. The waitress seemed interested, and Marcy asked for her phone number to follow up. The waitress seemed genuinely excited and gave Marcy her name/email/phone number and the check. Marcy was a little surprised to see a line of about four people waiting for the valet to bring their cars up. It turned out only one young man was valeting, and he was BUST-ING his BUTT, dripping sweat and sprinting back and forth with a SMILE on his face. As he pulled up in Marcy's silver sedan, she slipped him $5 and told him how impressive his hustle was. He thanked her and said, "I am just trying to earn enough money so I can afford to get my own apartment." Marcy quickly realized he would be an excellent business builder in her downline. She saw another revenue stream that could help out this young man before she even knew his name. She informed him she had been involved with a network marketing company for the past twenty-six years and had earned millions of dollars with her "part-time job." She invited the valet guy to her upcoming business class that was being held the upcoming Saturday. It is this mind-set that put Marcy at the highest rank of her company when she started twenty-six years ago at the age of forty-five. (She STARTED at forty-five years young!)

Challenges of Ice Cream Trucks

1. Spit Up and Give Way Too Much Information

Sometimes an Ice Cream Truck will talk themselves out of a great contact. Less is more: "I have some life-changing products you need in your life. I am person-ally inviting you to the class this Thursday." Sometimes circumstances dictate how much info you give. If you are on a three-hour plane ride and the person next to you keeps asking questions, keep giving information! If you are standing in line at the bank, it is not wise to give your entire presentation.

Corrective Action: Get a class on the books, and when you talk to people keep it short and invite them to the class. Also get a thirty-second, two-minute, and five-minute elevator speech prepared. This allows you to deliver information in an effective manner! Practice these elevator speeches in your home and then put them into action!

2. Once They Get the Sale They Are Done with the Prospect

I agree that for the most part, this business is a game of numbers. However, you may need to get less numbers if you build relationships with your customers and team members. An Ice Cream Truck can have the habit of moving on to the next one, when they really needed to invest some more time with the people they already have.

Corrective Action: Do at least one care call a week. A care call is a phone call that is just checking up on someone to strengthen a relationship and see if you can be of service. You should do care calls to your business builders as well as your customers. That would be fifty-two care calls for the year, and if your team is not that large, you have the luxury of touching base with every person in your organization!

3. Don't Listen Enough

An Ice Cream Truck has the tendency to say everything they wish, and it does not matter to them what the prospect has to say. It might not be that they don't care; it is just that they have not enhanced their skill of listening. YES, listening is a skill that can be improved.

If you are someone that is just waiting to blurt out your next words of wisdom while the other person is talking, without even acknowledging what they just said, you need to work on your listening craft.

Corrective Action: Learn and utilize the FORM method: gather information about their Family, Occupation, Recreation, and Motivation. The truth is, listening can give you so much valuable insight about someone. What makes them excited, what their intentions are for the business or product, and what is the leverage to get them over the hump!

Vehicle History Report

Vehicle: Electric Car

Mileage:
7,500 miles

Mechanic Notes:
The Electric Car is very efficient and doesn't waste energy. They use tech-savvy tools to help their business grow. They utilize webinars, Skype, Facetime, PowerPoint, video editor apps, graphic design apps, Google Chat, Facebook, Instagram, Excel, etc. They will Facebook Live a class for people that couldn't make it or are out of town. They analyze processes to make them easier and quicker, and are always trying to automate tasks.

Damage Report Diagnostic:
*No internal issues, here are the positive thought patterns of this vehicle:
- "My app tells me all the new rankers in my organization!"
- "Let's set up a webinar with this month's new people, and I will show them how to navigate the company's website. The people will be able to see everything I am doing on my screen from the comfort of their home."
- "Who doesn't have a smartphone?"

Previous Owners:
One

Warranty:
Has four years left or 100,000 miles of full bumper-to-bumper warranty.

Above or Below Retail Book Value:
The Electric Car can be very valuable. Ask your tech people if there are more efficient ways to get a hold of the masses. What are the new tech tools out there? Then share with your team. If you have something that takes up most of your time, ask an Electric Car to review the process to see if they have any ideas to simplify it. Work with an Electric Car to create graphics, websites, and content you both can use. An Electric Car can get overwhelmed with leads or warm markets; assist them with the follow-up! An Electric Car might know how to set up the Zoom call, but you can be the educator and expert on the call.

Here is a story of Jenna the Electric Car

Her heart was beating as she stood in line at Walgreens. Jenna stepped up to the cashier and placed the pregnancy test box on the counter. She and the clerk shared no words, but the tension was in the air for such a life-changing purchase. The Walgreens clerk picked up on Jenna's fear, and it was even further confirmed when Jenna had to pay for the test with a $10 bill and $6 in quarters. Money had been tight for Jenna and her husband, Michael. They both were extremely hard workers, but they couldn't get over the hump to stash away any savings. They bought a house last year and it somehow turned into an endless money sucker. The list for the first twelve months included $1,000 for a new washer and dryer, $1,500 roof repair for a leak,

$500 air conditioning repair, $1,500 new carpet that was NEEDED, $500 for a living room TV, $800 for a couch to watch the new TV, and the list keeps going, but we will stop there. Jenna and Michael had run up over $20,000 in credit card debt between the two of them.

Both Jenna and Michael owned and operated a brick-and-mortar business called You Need It, We Got It. It was a classic variety store that had everything from lawnmowers to back-to-school supplies. The store had been in Michael's family for forty years, and about five years ago Michael bought out the family and ran it with his wife. Business was good the first three years of owning it outright, but the last twenty-four months had been a challenge. Who knew a little tiny app named Amazon would cause so much trouble for Jenna and Michael. Suddenly everyone in their town was using the app to get everything. Michael would watch customers literally come in and scan an item on the Amazon app with their phone and walk out without buying anything. You Need It, We Got It couldn't compete with the pricing and ease of Amazon. Both Jenna and Michael knew their storefront was failing, debt was getting higher, and the bank account was always under $1,000 after the mortgage was paid.

Jenna finished the five-minute drive home with her Walgreens bag on the seat next to her. She slammed the front door behind her and jetted upstairs immediately. Jenna sat in her cold bathroom and bowed her head and whispered a prayer: "Dear God, if this is a positive test, PLEASE give me the strength and direction to provide for this child." Ten minutes later she was staring at the pee stick waiting for a life-altering + or -. It slowly faded into a +, and Jenna had every emotion she had ever felt hit her like a ten-foot wave in Hawaii. It was hard to describe feeling these feeling in a short time: joy, fear, regret, excitement, and responsibility. Over the next three months nothing had changed at Jenna's business, and you could see the weight of stress bearing down on Michael's shoulders.

Jenna had been using essential oils on and off for the past four years. She had a friend named Cassie that got her into them. Cassie's essential oil company of choice was a network marketing company, and at that point she was earning an extra $500 a month. Jenna called up Cassie to get the lowdown on the opportunity to pull in some extra cash to pay for utility bills. Four months pregnant now, Jenna had watched all of the company's compensation plan videos and trained up on the products. Jenna started hosting some at-home classes and was excited that people were receptive to the products. She got her first check of $215. Michael was swallowed in stress still, with a failing business and a child on the way, and didn't get too excited about the incoming money. He snapped at Jenna" "Two hundred dollars is great, honey, but it doesn't even cover half of a mortgage payment." Jenna, however, had tasted a small victory and was hungry for more.

Jenna made a conscious decision to get her family back on financial track. It was up to her to start up her network marketing business and build it large and fast. Her leverage was picturing her and her baby at a shelter because they lost the home. Jenna's leverage was so high that it gave her the drive to kick it into gear. She pulled out her iPad and began to write up a business game plan for her new oil business. Jenna realized that to build it quickly she needed to get in front of more people. Jenna was pretty tech savvy and began to brainstorm a list of effective and organized business tactics. Over the next thirty days Jenna worked six days a week and twelve-hour days. She would work a full day at the store and then go home and put three more hours into her oil business.

Jenna started up two YouTube channels. One was for making and sharing videos on the products; another was for the business side of network marketing. Jenna started sharing these YouTube videos with friends and family and got some interested in the products, and then the sales started trickling in.

The next step was setting up a booth at a job fair looking for new recruits, and she invested her paycheck back into a "sizzle call": she directed all the people she spoke with at the fair to call a 1-800 number and listen to her five-minute pre-recorded benefits of a home-based business.

Next up for Jenna was to brand herself on Facebook and Instagram. Jenna read up on the best way to utilize these tools. She found that she needed to post funny stories and pictures throughout the week and sprinkle in her product ads naturally and with an air of fun. Jenna had slow traction in the beginning, but as the months went on there was more interest in her posts and much more interaction with her followers.

Then Jenna started up a health blog, and she knew she needed to connect with a large number of people. Her blog didn't have too many viewers, but she stayed consistent with at least three articles a month. Again, she realized that each blog entry couldn't be, "Buy my products," so she added value to her readers with a wide range of great content! Jenna's team and customers started to grow a little.

Jenna knew it was time to figure out how to do a webinar, and she had ten of her business builders attend the online event. She had created a PowerPoint and was able to do the webinar so it showed her and her PowerPoint for all to see. It was a product-driven PowerPoint, but the intention was all business. Jenna showed how easy it was to give the presentation and then sent it out to all ten business builders that were on the call. Jenna was smart enough to realize that she needed to get duplicatable tools in her business builders' hands.

Jenna needed more leads and took her paycheck again and purchased five thousand leads for an email campaign. She figured out how to build a website on Wix.com for $200. She took the email campaign and sent out a nicely done image that had the prospect click on her website for a free essential oil class video. When the prospect clicked to website she had set up a landing page to capture their info in the database, to be used later.

With all the webinars, website launches, email campaigns, blogging, YouTube videos, and Facebook events/groups/posts, Jenna started to see some real momentum. This was PERFECT timing because she was getting ready to welcome a baby girl in a month from now.

Jenna was waddling around and talking to everyone about the health benefits of the oils, and she still realized that using her tech skills to connect with thousands of people was how she was going to save her house and keep her family out of that shelter that still haunted her dreams.

Michael started coming around a little when he saw the last check of $750, but he knew they were running out of time. Michael sat down his nine-month-pregnant wife and told her he had crunched all the numbers and with the expense of the baby (can you believe it's $4,000 to have a baby in a hospital!!??) and increased payroll at the store with Jenna taking some time off, that they only had four months left of credit card debt before they couldn't afford the car and mortgage payment.

Jenna survived the miracle that is childbirth and was finally able to hold her "why" in her motherly hands. All this did was add fuel to this new mamma's fire. She recorded a video about using the oils and her baby and put it up on her blog like any other day. By the morning something different had happened, and the blog had been shared over two-hundred times on Facebook. She had a flood of new emails from prospects choosing to get the products. Jenna had a monstrous month and signed up thirty new customers. The check of $2,200 that rolled in was like a knight in shining armor riding a horse in slow motion as he swings his sword fiercely to take down a dragon.

The momentum didn't stop, and Jenna connected with each of these new people via Facetime and Skype. Jenna knew she needed to build trust with her new customers. Luckily, with the technology, it didn't matter what state they lived in; she was able to have a face-to-face conversation in the Internet world.

Twelve months later Jenna was supporting her family like a #LadyBoss. Her checks ranged from $4,000–$8,000 a month. Michael was still grinding out the hours breaking even with the variety store. One day, after a long day at work he came home to find Jenna on the couch with a big smile on her face. Michael somehow knew the news before she even said it. She flashed a + sign on the pregnancy test stick and gave Michael a big hug and whispered, "Emma is going to be a big sister." This time it was different for Michael and Jenna. They got to enjoy the moment and gift God was giving them. There was less financial stress and, in turn, their marriage had become a true partnership.

Jenna scanned the cakes at the bakery for Emma's second birthday. She couldn't believe she had a toddler and a three-month-old. Her essential oil business was booming from all the tech and tools she was using. Her checks were consistently $12,000 a month—which for Michael and Jenna felt like a million dollars a month. One new test Jenna had to deal with was running a business with no sleep, a kid tugging on her leg all day, a house that got messed up five minutes after she cleaned it spotless, and taking calls with a screaming baby in her hand. Jenna now had to attempt to run her empire while keeping two small children alive, but she wouldn't change it for the world. She often thought back on the prayer where she asked God, "Dear God, if this is a positive test, PLEASE give me the strength and direction to provide for this child." Jenna's leverage was so great, and combined with her tech-savvy business game plan, she couldn't be stopped. She is now asking Michael for a third little angel—and he knows Jenna gets anything she sets her mind to.

Challenging Traits of Electric Cars

1. Thinks Everyone Is as Smart as Them

Electric Cars sometimes forget that most people do not know how to create a webinar, use Dropbox for large files, create Excel formulas, create websites, etc. Even going to a website, clicking "Order Now" and then continuing the sign-up process is a challenge for some people. I have heard several times, "What's a URL?" or "I don't have a computer or email." To an Electric Car that is SHOCKING!! How could you survive without Wi-Fi, a laptop, or email??

Corrective Action: Get your prospect or customer on the phone or in person and walk them through like a baby. You need to remember that not everyone is great with links and computer sign-ups. They may need to fill out the form old-school style. For that reason, my mentor has taught me to always carry a handwritten sign-up form. You also have to remember that technology can be unreliable sometimes. Be patient with the technology-challenged people of the world!

2. Loses Sight of the Belly-to-Belly Relationship Aspect

An Electric Car can get lost in the virtual world sometimes. They can lose sight of the most effective way to strengthen a relationship, which is face-to-face.

Corrective Action: Use the tech world or the phone to get belly-to-belly. I like to call this tactic tech to touch. Use your technology to get you an actual face-to-face encounter. Use your tools to make initial contact and stay in touch, with the goal of meeting or connecting in person. There is something powerful that takes place when you have dinner with someone or are invited into someone's home. Remember to utilize tech to touch.

3. Takes Out the Personalization

The Electric Car's focus is to automate everything. This is a great idea, and for the most part it is going to make their business run effectively and efficiently. However, there are some times when the Electric Car will need to put a personal touch on things. For example, with email drips/campaigns (automated spaced-out emails) the Electric Car may have met a new team builder and had a great conversation and plugged their info into their drip system to start receiving. However, when the team builder opens it up, it may not have any personal touch on it from their conversation, making the team builder feel like they are not really valued.

Corrective Action: Taking the time to personally write a message to the new builder and put a personal touch on it from the conversation will go a long way in strengthening the relationship. After the personal touch email the Electric Car can go ahead and start the email drips.

Vehicle: Ambulance

Mileage:
8,000 miles

Mechanic Notes:
The Ambulance truly makes a difference and helps people. "You need help at the expo? I'm there!!" Ambulances don't know where they are helping next. They just truly deliver when you need it. An Ambulance is genuine and cares about the relationship over money. They create a safe team helping environment.

Damage Report Diagnostic:
*No internal issues, here are the positive thought patterns of this vehicle:
- "How is the family doing?"
- "How can I support and assist you?"
- "It's not about the money; I just wish you to be happy."

Previous Owners:
One

Warranty:
Has four years left under warranty or 100,000 miles of full bumper-to-bumper warranty.

Above or Below Retail Book Value:
Ambulances are well above retail book value. Value the relationship with your Ambulance. Build trust between you and this team member. Send them birthday and

holiday cards. Give them recognition and gratitude when they rank up. Stay in constant communication with your Ambulances. They value their people and are tapped into their needs and can direct you on how to assist. They are true leaders in network marketing. They are going to build long-lasting relationships. They will always do the right thing. They care more about the person than the commission. They thrive off making people better and developing leaders. The ambulance's heart gets filled when their people rank up and have success. Take some more time scheduling training events for your ambulance's team. Invest your time, effort, and resources as much as you can into this team member. The benefits will be blissful and reciprocal.

Here is a story of Maddy the Ambulance

Max was holding back tears as he sifted through old pictures from his mom's albums. It felt different being in her house with her gone. He called his sister, Kate: "Hey, can you swing by Mom's place? I need some help building these picture boards for the funeral . . . Okay, Sis, see you soon." The pictures were bringing back a flood of memories and emotions. One picture that Max couldn't stop staring at was a picture from 1978. It was his whole family: sister Kate, dad Samuel, and mom Madelyn, who everyone called "Maddy," helping serve food on Thanksgiving. Max was only four years old in the picture, with an apron on, handing out biscuits. Kate was filling up glasses of lemonade, Dad was cutting turkey, and Maddy was pouring gravy on a homeless person's plate with THE biggest smile on her face. This was a tradition that Max didn't like doing at the time. However, as he got older his respect for his mother grew every day. The selflessness and care she had for people was unmatched. When Max was seventeen he lost his dad to a heart attack. Maddy raised Max and Kate with love and care until last week when she lost her battle with cancer.

Kate pulled into her mother's driveway and just sat in the car for five minutes with her head on the steering wheel to collect herself. She walked in to find Max sprawled out on the living room floor with pictures and albums everywhere. "Kate, look at this one," Max said with a smile, flashing the photo of all four of them huddled around a tiny golden retriever puppy. "That's the day I picked out our first family dog. Goldy was such a sweetheart!" As Kate started to go through pictures, she began to see all the lives her mother had touched. "Mom was always helping people. I think one of the picture boards should be of her philanthropic values. We're not short of pictures for that! Here are some of her helping build houses in Ecuador, volunteering to read to the hospital's terminally ill children, organizing a toy drive before Christmas for the families who lost their home in that huge tornado." Kate couldn't believe how giving her mom Maddy was. Kate knew her mom was the best, but when she started going through her life, she realized it was all about helping others. She cracked a smile when she remembered how pissed off she was when her mom sold her toys at their garage sale to raise money for their next-door neighbor who had lost his job, back in 1983. Although Maddy wasn't rich while raising her kids she gave as much as she could to those who needed it. Kate had known the day was coming when she would lose her mother, but having it finally arrive was crushing.

The first hour of the funeral had Max and Kate

taken back a little. The church held 120 people and it was standing room only before the speaking even began. Max addressed everyone and at the end asked if anyone would like to share a story of Maddy. Fifteen people began to line up at the bottom of the stage, and each had their own story about how Maddy had touched their heart and supported them. It became clear to Max and Kate just how big of a reach Maddy had throughout the community. The stories were as small as a woman telling of when her husband, Lenny, was ill and on bed rest. She looked out the window to see Maddy mowing her lawn, knowing it was Lenny who had pride in his lawn always looking the best. The woman relayed how big the smile was on Lenny's face knowing his yard was still looking great! The stories and memories kept coming from the crowd, and the service went two hours past the ending time.

Three weeks passed since the funeral, and one day Max got a call from his mom's lawyer, Eric. Eric explained there were some items the law firm needed to discuss with Max and his sister. The next day Kate and Max were at the office and were escorted to a large board room with twenty really nice leather chairs and a huge glossy dark-wood table. They took a seat and waited for Eric, the lawyer, not knowing what this was all about. Eric walked in, and after the handshakes, he got right to business. "Are you familiar with your mom's business, Health Nut Company?" Eric asked with a straight face. Max replied, "Yeah, that is the company my mom buys all the healthy stuff from. They have vitamins, supplements, really organic and holistic products. I still use some of the products my mom gave me." Eric went on to explain that Health Nut Company was a network marketing company and that Madelyn had built a great organization of over two thousand people. In Madelyn's will she laid out how she had set up a trust for the residual income of her commission checks to go into a bank account and be split between Kate and Max. It wasn't lottery money, but it was about $8,000 for them to split each month. Eric pulled out a letter from Maddy to her children regarding this inheritance.

Dear Sweet Kate and Mad Max,

Both of you know when you were teens I had my first bout with cancer. It was at that time when I started looking at health and wellness. It led me to the Health Nut Company, and I started using the products myself. I loved them so much I started recommending them to people I thought needed them. It was a lifestyle change and one I needed. By me sharing and educating on health, it led to an unexpected paycheck that began to grow, and quite frankly has allowed me to travel and donate my time and money for those in need. Health Nut's policies and procedures allow me to give my organization away in my will as a legacy. I envision both of you doing amazing things with this money. Take care of your families first, and assist others with the rest. Remember, each day I didn't know who needed my help, but the Lord always brought them into my life, and you will know in your heart where you can help. Don't think I was keeping this a secret from you. I tried MANY times to get you both involved. I believe Max's response was, "I don't do pyramid schemes, Mom." If you choose to continue to

grow the organization, get with Trudy. She is
a top leader and will show you the ropes! Eric
will go over all the details with you.

Always remember mamma is proud of you
both, and your father and I are looking down
on you with love from above!

Love,
Mamma

Weeks later Max and Kate were embracing their new business they had inherited. Max was the dreamer and ideas guy, and Kate was the action/make-things-happen girl. They were a great team. They went through their mom's office things and found a "customers" folder. This folder had hundreds of names and info about Maddy's Health Nut customers. Max and Kate noticed their mom would send birthday gifts to most of her organization, she would send cards for married couples' anniversaries, she had her business builders' goals in their own section. It was obvious their mom took an interest in each person and made them feel special. Kate and Max reached out to their new downline, and the response was excellent from the customers, who had been working with Maddy for over a decade. They all would comment on how helpful Maddy was. Although Kate and Max would be doing this business part time, they both saw a future of continuing their mom's legacy of spreading health and wellness to the world.

Challenging Traits of Ambulances

1. Give Away the Farm

The Ambulance cares and gives so much, sometimes to a fault! People can and will take advantage of this kindness. If the Ambulance has a product and someone asks if they can have it, they don't hesitate, and sometimes they don't even charge them for it! Just because you care and choose to help people, it does not mean that you give everything away. If an Ambulance has a prospect that desires to go to the convention, a challenging trait is that the Ambulance will buy their plane ticket, meals, lodging, etc.

Corrective Action: Set a limit of $50 a month in giveaways, or an amount that you are comfortable with. If someone REALLY has interest in going to the convention they will find a way to get there. YOU do NOT need to be their financial savior. Come up with solutions to cut costs for them, but don't pay their way. If you have product someone needs, charge them what you paid. If people get things for free once, they expect it going forward. Another key element is that if someone ponies up $300 to go to a personal growth seminar, they usually get more out of it. If you pay their $300 ticket it is a free roll, and they might not be as focused and driven to get value out of the event. You need to set limits and boundaries that work for you. Don't get me wrong, getting someone to your company's convention is excellent, so maybe make it a GRAND prize for a contest you run; that means the person actually had to earn it. Your resources are valuable, so invest them wisely.

2. Overextend Themselves to Burnout

It is very difficult for an Ambulance to say no, because they choose to help everyone all the time. They could have a prospect ask them to help out at a booth at the state fair and end up working four straight ten-hour days. An Ambulance can work so hard trying to please everyone they get burnt out and can shut down altogether.

Corrective Action: Set a limit that Sundays are your recharge day. Create opportunities for your downline to step up. For example, if there is an all-day expo, try to empower your team to take this as an opportunity to enhance their skills and get out there! If you are asked to help out but you know it will overextend you, either (A) Say it doesn't work with your schedule or (B) Search through your team for someone who would be a good fit to assist the request. It will be tough for an Ambulance to say no, but make sure it works for YOU.

3. They Don't Know How to Utilize Their Comp Plan

Ambulances are truly focused on building relationships and assisting others. But if they don't know and utilize their compensation plan, they could be leaving thousands of dollars on the table.

Corrective Action: Find an expert and ask for a one-on-one teaching, so you can ask questions. Then teach a comp plan class to help you retain the knowledge and learn how to apply it. It is amazing that once you start teaching something, you really dive into it to understand it yourself. Also have an upline member look at your organization to see where they feel your efforts should go, or if there are any obvious holes in your organization. You may be able to get your hands on videos that have been made about the comp plan. At least get the basics down so you can HELP others utilize the plan. Remember if you make more money, that can, in turn, allow you to help more people! You might even become like a Mark Zuckerberg, who has pledged 99 percent of his Facebook stock to charity.

Vehicle: BULLDOZER

Mileage:
7,000 miles

Mechanic Notes:
The Bulldozer has a level head and can't be stopped. It is consistent. It stays the course and does not have the emotional ups and downs. It knows that you just need to keep going. With all the chaos in front of it, it just keeps pushing until it clears the path, moving all the negativity and roadblocks off the streets. A Bulldozer is excellent at seeing the long-term vision. It utilizes vision boards, goals, manifesting, and believing before it happens!

Damage Report Diagnostic:
*No internal issues, here are the positive thought patterns of this vehicle:
- "No one showed up for my class . . . Time to book another one!"
- "I will one day hit the rank of my dreams. Just need to take it one day at a time."
- "I will take this new change within the company as a challenge!"

Previous Owners:
One

Warranty:
Has four years left under warranty or 100,000 miles of full bumper-to-bumper warranty.

Above or Below Retail Book Value:
Bulldozers are well above retail book value. Give them the keys to drive. They are going to the top with or without you, but you can speed up their business growth. All the obstacles in their way are not going to stop them. This is the person you assist in any way possible. Keep constant and open communication with this team member. This is the person you hop on a plane for and travel to their city. The bulldozer is someone with whom you take the time to create business plans and brainstorm marketing strategies. If a bulldozer would like a PowerPoint, help them create one. A bulldozer will utilize the resources you give them. They put ideas into action. If a bulldozer requests a three-way call, get excited and jump at the opportunity. If you see a great new handout about your product or company, make the investment and send your bulldozer ten of them. Build and value this relationship with high regard, and it will benefit both of you.

Here is a short story about a Bulldozer named Ellie

This night had been twenty years in the making. Ellie tried on her third dress in the last thirty minutes trying to make sure everything was perfect, but you would think she would already know what to wear after envisioning this night over one hundred times. Her husband Vince finished buttoning up his suit and adjusting the bow tie. Unlike Ellie, he didn't think this day would ever come and actually felt guilty about fighting and holding Ellie back for the first thirteen years of her home-based business. As they were driving to the venue for the awards night for his wife's company he was having flashbacks of how nasty he was in the beginning years. Thoughts of,

"Ellie, I love you, but you are wasting your time."

"Me and you aren't the people that get to be in the 1 percent."

"Quit wasting our money on those stupid ra-ra-ra seminars."
"We don't have enough connections, and I don't desire you to harass my friends and family."

"You need to quit this pyramid scheme and get a REAL second job; we need the money."

Vince tried to get these thoughts out of his head and focus on making sure Ellie wasn't nervous for her speech. "Darling, do you know what you are going to say when you accept the award on stage?" Vince said in a calm voice.

"I am going to do what I always do and just talk from the heart. The Lord will guide me on what needs to be said," Ellie said with full confidence.

Ellie and Vince were seated at a round table with eight others, eating a perfectly cooked steak dinner. Ellie looked around this black-tie affair and saw so many lives she had touched and relationships she had built over the last twenty years. In that time, she had seen other members zoom to the top and many others fizzle out. Suddenly, a familiar voice took the stage and began talking into the microphone for the next introduction. It was the founder of the company, Mr. Anderson.

"I have chosen to personally introduce our next award. This one is special to me. I'm very excited to announce Ellie as our newest Platinum Rank in the company, but first I will tell you a little about Ellie and some memories I have. The first time I met her was at our company's convention eighteen years ago. Believe it or not there were forty-one people there! A far cry from the fifteen thousand attending this year. This woman came up to me, and I will never forget it, she said, "Hello, Mr. Anderson, my name is Ellie. I have been with the company for two years now, and I am not turning a profit, but I choose to thank you for creating this opportunity for me." I was stunned and asked her why she was thanking me if she wasn't making any money. She replied, "I know this isn't a get-rich-quick scheme, and it takes some people longer to build an organization. I am not going to quit until I am a Platinum in your company. I am not sure how long it will take me, but it will happen." Mr. Anderson was starting to tear up a little at this point, and before he couldn't keep himself together, he introduced Ellie to the stage for her speech. The crowd applauded, and Ellie walked up the six stairs to the stage, shook some hands of the executive team, and took the flowers from the founder. She stepped up to the microphone:

"Thank you, Mr. Anderson. I remember that conversation as well. This award is not just for me. It is for all the people out there that believe in something well before it happens, even when all of the closest people in your life doubt you and try to hold you back. I have always constantly told myself they just didn't see the vision I see. I actually wish to thank my husband, Vince. He doesn't know this, but he is the reason I got into the business. See, I was forty-two years old at the time and overheard a conversation my husband was having with our accountant. I heard Vince say, "We already took the equity out of the home. What is the penalty to take all my 401K out? Okay, let's do it." I never told him I overheard that he was liquidating our retirement money. Instead, I started researching how I could take matters into my own hands and live comfortably in our older age. My studying led me to residual income, and the only way I could get it was to be a movie star, make a rap album [the crowd erupts in laughter], or become a network marketer. It was then I made the decision and NEVER looked back. Yes, there were brief times when I asked myself, 'Will I ever make it?' and, 'Why am I doing this?' but I just knew in my heart that this was my path. I desire everyone to know that you don't need to be the best closer, or have the best graphics, or be the best speaker. I am none of those. What I am is consistent. I stand before you after twenty years and over 480 classes (2 per month for twenty years), eight comp plan changes, eleven CEOs, one hundred Webinars, 500 three-way calls, and have talked to over two thousand people about our products. I am sixty-two years young now and plan on living well into my eighties. Vince and I plan on going to Seattle's Seafair every year for the next twenty years, and we are going to have Christmas in the Bahamas this year. I have never been out of the country, and we have our tickets booked for Italy in March. We are going to do what we choose to do for the next couple decades. I also wish to thank my team for making this possible. I would not be here without them. I love our products and our company, and I thank you, Mr. Anderson, for this opportunity you have given me."

Challenging Traits of Bulldozers

1. Rude or Pushy

Sometimes the Bulldozer desires it so bad they will get aggressive toward their customers to become business builders. A Bulldozer at times can tear someone down who doesn't choose to go to the company's convention. They see the vision for other people and get angry when the other person does not see it.

Corrective Action: You need to meet them where they are at. That means if they are a customer that chooses to just get product, don't force them to host a webinar. If you have a business builder that wishes to only do it part time, don't harass them to host five events a month. You need to get into their world and see what works for them. Determine how you can best assist your customers and business builders. I agree that at some point you need to give a little push to people to get them out of their comfort zone, and after that they thank you. You need to gauge where people are at and the best way to do that is to talk to them and listen! They will give you the answers. If a prospect tells you they desire to quit their full-time job and will do whatever it takes. That is the person you can push and be all over. If a product/service tells you they have no interest in doing anything on the business side, then support them with product knowledge and company assistance. I always let my product users know the door is open at any time if they would like to get some product paid for. It is so much more powerful if it is their idea to earn income and not yours! Let them come around, and be a safe and supportive person in their life. Again, meet them where they are, and not where you need them to be!

2. Not Being Duplicatable

Some Bulldozers have studied everything there is to know about the product or service. When they do a presentation and drop knowledge effortlessly, it can be intimidating for a business builder who watches the presentation. They say, "I could never be that smart, or talented, or memorize all of that." Bulldozers may build in ways others can't, like doing something that costs a ton of money. Not everyone has a large budget to build their business. A bulldozer also may have built their business in a unique way, such as having a very successful blog and then introducing their product or service. Something like that is not very duplicatable for the average person.

Corrective Action: First, if your presentations read like encyclopedias, you also need to have a duplicatable version for your business builders: a fun, simple presentation that anyone can prepare and present. There is the old acronym, KISS, which stands for Keep It Simple Stupid. In this business, simplicity is what can drive growth. Also, a great way to take stress off your team so they do not need to be the expert is to get as many tools and material in their hands as you can. Give them a package of great resources and tools they can use in their business. It will help shorten the learning curve and is very duplicatable. We send out a welcome packet and email to all new members. In the email, there are videos on how to order, how to get on auto-ship, the company's phone number for issues, etc. Other great duplicatable tools include scripts, videos, books, three-way calls, and webinars.

3. Social Media Disaster

Bulldozers know they are going to the top, and one way they choose to build is through social media. However, the problem is they don't do it correctly and naturally. EVERY post is about the business or product. They constantly post their link and it screams, "Buy my product! ANYONE, PLEASE, BUY, BUY, BUY! I NEED THIS!!" They don't make it personal and have no connection to the people that read it. Social media is becoming an art, and you need to know how to play the game.

Corrective Action: Make sure to promote the lifestyle in a natural way online. Don't just post your link; turn it into a relatable story. Pictures are great, and videos are even better! Stories sell and connect people to you. It can't be business, business, business; a solid ratio is four personal posts to one business post. Be a positive influence on someone's timeline, add value, and know that even if you don't get "likes," people are reading what you post! This advice doesn't just apply to the virtual world. Work on building a relationship with someone. You don't always have to bring up the business the first time you meet a new person. Remember to also use tech to touch. Use the technology to get face-to-face!

Custom Build Your Vehicle

Grab a pen and paper. I'll wait. Go. You have now read about nine different personalities/vehicles. But I am going to let you in on a secret: A person can be a combination of several cars. You can have a member in your team that talks to everyone about their product (Ice Cream Truck trait), constantly cheats their way to the top (Race Car trait), and complains and gossips about everything (Lemon trait). This member could be 50 percent Ice Cream Truck, 30 percent race car, and 20 percent Lemon.

As someone who was drawn to math as a kid and was an accountant for over seven years, one thing I understand is percentages. I think and talk in percentages. If my wife asks me if I am hungry, I'll say, "I am about 67 percent hungry," a.k.a., I could eat, but I am not starving. Percentages give an accurate account of everything.

Think about yourself for a minute. You need to be truthful and honest in this evaluation. Take your pen and paper and write down what you currently are right now. Take four of the vehicles and break down what you are in percentages that combined equal 100 percent. My example below is what I think would make a dynamite professional network marketer. Part Ambulance, Ice Cream Truck, Bulldozer, and Electric Car, which means they care about relationships, they talk to new prospects about their company, they keep pushing through adversity, and they have some techy skills.

If you know that you have some Tow Truck traits, for example, you struggle with taking action and doing the follow-up. The good news is YOU can change your percentages and traits. If your leverage changes in your life, it can bust you out of your comfort zone and change your habits. If your spouse loses their job and you can't pay the mortgage thirty days from now, your leverage to do the follow-up increases.

After filling out what you are currently, fill out what you choose to be going forward. Still be true to yourself on this exercise. Thankfully, we are all different. There is not one combination of vehicles that is proven to be the best. When I see my company's top leaders, they all have different stories and personalities. For the most part they were able to get to the top by building a business that worked for them.

% Percentages %

Examples Combination: Going Forward	What are you currently?	What do you choose to be?
30 % Ambulance	1. ___ _____	1. ___ _____
40 % Ice Cream Truck	2. ___ _____	2. ___ _____
20 % Bulldozer	3. ___ _____	3. ___ _____
10 % Tesla	4. ___ _____	4. ___ _____

CHAPTER 5

Going the Extra Mile

These days a Yelp review can make or break a company. If an auto repair shop has a two-star average or a slew of negative reviews, the Yelpers won't even think about getting a repair done at this establishment.

Case in point, I recently had my carpets cleaned. Yes, I found the company on Yelp and they had over two thousand reviews and a 4.5–5 star rating. After they finished the cleaning, I wasn't happy with the job. (We had a coffee stain that looked the same after they were done.) Two days after the carpet cleaning, I received a text from the owner asking how everything looked. I explained I was a little disappointed that they couldn't do more with the stain. He apologized and told me he could give me a $25 refund or they could come out and try to work on the stain some more. The company came back out and used a special coffee remover recipe. The stain came out and the company did not charge me for coming back out. It instantly changed my mind on their service and company. That they were willing to go the extra mile to satisfy their customer spoke volumes.

Take a second, and pretend that in your network marketing business each and every person you sign up to purchase product or is interested in the business has the power to give YOU a Yelp review. What would they say? How many stars would you average for your rating? If you did this and did the follow-up like my carpet cleaning company, it would change how your customers view you. You are always going to have situations go wrong for your members; it is how you respond to the issues that they will remember. If someone has a complaint or issue, do your best to take care of them. This is YOUR business, and these are YOUR customers. Make them feel special and that you care about their experience. They in turn will likely be more comfortable sharing their experience and promoting you and your products/services. Have some fun and pretend EVERYONE can give you a Yelp review, and take that review very seriously.

Now that you realize the power of taking care of YOUR customers, let us look at how to utilize leverage. This could be the most important piece you take from this book. If you put focus on leverage, you can grow your business.

CHAPTER 6

Leverage

A few years after dating my girlfriend Kortni, she dragged me to a Tony Robbins event. The only thing I knew about him was that he was the Giant from the comedy *Shallow Hal.* I dragged my feet a little about going to a "self-help" seminar. The tickets were a couple thousand dollars PER TICKET! However, after three days of massaging strangers, jumping, clapping, and walking on fire, I realized I was learning from one of the greatest personal growth mentors of our time.

A key piece that I learned at this event, which is a must to understand in network marketing, is *LEVERAGE.* A simple way to summarize leverage would be this: if you were going to get $1,000,000 to cold call thirty people, you would do it in a heartbeat. If you were going to get $1 to cold call thirty people, you most likely would not do it. There is very high leverage to call the people for a million, and the leverage is very low to call for $1. Here's another example: If your family would be evicted and homeless unless you signed up two people this month, you absolutely would talk to all your contacts to avoid the severe negative consequence, which has high leverage. If your family would not be able to eat potato chips for a week unless you signed two people up this month, there is low leverage and they can skip the chips.

You need to look at yourself and decide what is your highest leverage for your business. It could be that your family is about to lose the house and file bankruptcy, and that leverage makes you work harder than you ever have. It could be that you love helping people improve themselves, and the joy you get out of it carries extremely high leverage. For me, it was that I hated my accounting job with a passion. My leverage to be successful in network marketing was that I did not desire to go back to my boss and cubicle. When I was at one of my lowest moments with my corp. job, I wrote myself a note. I revisit this note when I do not feel like hosting another class or when I get discouraged with my MLM business. The note says this:

> *Remember this moment. Channel my disgust and anger toward my current job into passion and fuel for my network marketing business. Think about how miserable I am and focus on having my freedom and a better life.*

I recall being so fed up and present in the moment when I wrote that, and I made a conscious effort not to allow myself to ever forget how I felt. That is my leverage to keep pushing forward and not be bound to two weeks of vacation and several bosses breathing down my neck fifty hours a week. You need to find your leverage and make that a focal point; this is why you do what you do. You will NEED this when you are teaching two classes a week, sending out welcome packets, hearing the word NO a thousand times, being labeled, judged, and doubted, and second-guessing if you should keep with MLM.

You will also need to figure out your team members' leverage. I have a business builder whose husband makes great money, and they have a great home and happy family. I asked her questions on what was going to make her continue doing network marketing. Her reply was, "I set a goal of a rank, and I choose to finish it." My fear is that this is not high enough leverage to fully push her out of her comfort zone to do what it takes to make the rank she desires. Anyone can do this business part time and make a couple hundred dollars a month. It takes high leverage to put in the work that needs to be done to start earning $20,000 a month. Time will tell for this team member, who I cherish dearly, and I continue to support her the best I can.

> ***Learn*** *your business builders'* ***leverage*** *and remind them of it. Make it a* ***focal point.***

Now that you understand that high leverage can help you conquer tasks you don't wish to do, let us look at a specific type of extra effort that needs to be given to certain people.

CHAPTER 7

High Performance

There are going to be times with all these different cars and personalities that some cars will need high-performance tires, high-end gas, custom shocks, etc. These vehicles may take more time and money, but taking the time to put on the high-performance tires means that this car can turn better at high speeds. Equating this to network marketing, at some point you are going to come across someone who needs more attention, asks for more resources, likes monthly calls with you, and asks a million small detail questions. Don't just dismiss this person. Take some extra time to mold this person into a leader. They may transform from being a high-maintenance team member to a high-performing team member.

CHAPTER 8

Brand Name

When you think of some brands you associate it with luxury or well made vehicles. You might have never even owned that brand, but you trust it. In network marketing that is similar to a very powerful tool, third-party edification. It is a true game changer if you can understand it, and how to effectively use it. This is edifying someone else as the expert. I could tell my friends and family something all day long, but they know me, so what I say doesn't always carry as much weight. However, they could hear the same thing from someone I edified as an expert who is a total stranger and it hits home for them. Edify your upline to your prospects and get them together. It is mind expanding sometimes when you see your prospects hear the same thing you have been saying for years but it clicks when it come from the "expert" and not you. Third party edification is HUGE in this business.

CHAPTER 9

Daytona 500 (Contests)

The Daytona 500 is the most prestigious and recognized car race in the United States. It was first held in 1959 in Daytona Beach Florida, and has been held there every year since. The race is five hundred miles and two hundred laps. Unfortunately, it also is known for taking the life of Dale Earnhardt in a crash during the final lap of the race. For many, NASCAR is boring to watch, but can you imagine being a driver in one of those cars zipping around at two hundred miles per hour with fifty other cars trying to pass you and cut you off. Some thrive off this competitiveness—which in some cases rings true in network marketing.

One way you can nurture this competitiveness and have it work to your favor is by having contests for your team builders. I have had great success creating contests in my organization. For some people, it just lights something under them. The same people who might normally coast through a month, respond well if you give them a challenge with the possibility of winning a prize.

For my business, I ran three separate contests for three consecutive months. My company ideally wishes associates to follow a three-step process of (1) Introducing a potential customer to our product, (2) having them sign up with a membership, and (3) getting them on the company's monthly auto-ship program.

With this easy three-step process I made the contest for the first month to introduce our product to as many people as possible. The person who received the most no's in the month won the prize. I had people plant as many seeds in this first contest as possible. This contest was based off of a book I read called *Go for No!* by Richard Fenton and Andrea Waltz. It changes your relationship with the word no: it is *NOT* a bad thing. Enough no's lead to finding a yes, so you are encouraged to go for no! (One disclaimer I need to put in here is although most of my team loved their new relationship with the word no, I had one distributor who is a master manifester, and it was very difficult for her to continue this challenge and consciously put out there that she desired no's. She instead changed her goal to "Go for future leaders." She did this because for the first time after holding a class, no one at the classes signed up for back-to-back classes, two times in a row.)

Contest number two was to sign up as many people in the month as you can. Contest number three was to get someone on auto-ship who was not currently on it.

In summary, the concept of these three contests was to plant as many seeds as possible, sign up customers, and then get them on auto-ship. It brought focus and attention to all three of our company's main goals.

As far as the prizes for your contests, you can decide what you are comfortable with. I always recommend tying in the prizes to something related to your company. Another tip is to have a raffle for ANYONE that participated, if they got one no, signed up one person, or got one person on auto-ship, they could win a prize. For my contests, I talked to my leaders and asked them what moves them. Is it trips, cash, an iPad mini, company product, etc. Ask your leaders what they would like and decide what you are comfortable giving. Remember, though, that these are investments in your business and can be included as expenses for tax deductions.

To recap, find some areas where your team needs to focus more, and run a contest for it!

CHAPTER 10

Headlights

Headlights on a car help you see when you are driving and it's pitch-black out—because everyone knows you can't drive if you can't see well enough. The same goes for network marketing: vision is needed! I continue to see all these great minds echo a similar theme of goal setting, affirmations, manifesting, and the power of intention. For goal setting, I don't just mean thinking of a couple of long-term goals; I am talking, these people write their goals down and read them every morning out loud, and they have vision boards in their closets and empowering sayings on their bathroom mirrors.

Not convinced? Here are some interesting facts on goal setting:

*3 out of 100 adults will write their goals down on paper.

*People with written goals are 50 percent more likely to achieve than people without goals.

*A Harvard study suggests 83 percent of people do not have goals.

*Sharing your goals with a close confidant is proven to increase the chances of reaching your goals.

*92 percent of New Year's goals fail by January 15th.

*Specific goals that are time bound and measurable work best.

*Setting goals is the first step of making the invisible visible.

-Information credited to GoalBand: http://www.goalband.co.uk/goal-achievement-facts.html.

My personal take on these powerful universe tactics is to put focus on something, and when there is focus on something your brain is more alert and aware of anything that has to do with it.

For example, have you ever looked at buying a new car and searched the thousands of choices? Then when you bought the car that was all you saw on the road, and you thought to yourself, "Wow, I didn't know how many people drove a Jeep Grand Cherokee." The SAME principal goes for goals, intentions, and affirmations—putting focus on an intended outcome.

The more you see, smell, taste, and verbalize something, the more real it is and the more you focus on it. Do what you feel comfortable with, but bring more focus to what your outcome is.

Chapter 11

Gas in the Tank

At least in 2016, when we drive, fuel is consumed, and we need to refill our tanks with gas for our vehicles to run. (Although I am sure ten years from now most cars will be rechargeable, and at that time I will rename this segment!) Just like a car that won't go when the tank is empty, YOU need to refill your gas tank to keep yourself running. To do that in network marketing you need to constantly fill your tank with personal growth. One of the most effective ways to do this is by attending network marketing events. A tip for these events is to get your team members there! I've attended MANY in my day, and it always energizes me and fills up my tank. This refueling usually last two months, and then I need another refill. That's when I watch an inspirational video, or read a book to enhance my skills and knowledge.

Why is this important? Well, the fact is most of the actions we need to take in this business are skills that can be learned! And by improving our skills, we are fueling our ability to go further in the business. Think about it: listening is a skill, presenting and speaking are skills, learning how to work a prospect list is a skill! Keep sharpening your skills, working on yourself to become a better person and leader, and filling your gas tank up to get your car moving forward again!

CHAPTER 12

Windshield Wipers

When you're driving and it's pouring down rain, what do you do? Slow down a little and flip on your wipers so you remove the obstacles (raindrops) from your windshield and see more clearly. Similarly, there are some moments in life that you can remember the exact moment when something clicked and you could see with clarity. Here is one of mine:

My wife and I had talked about me being able to quit the corporate world if we got our network marketing checks up to a certain amount. On that quest, we had the opportunity to attend an event in Texas called the ANMP, Association of Network Marketing Professionals. We tend to jump on any opportunity to attend personal growth events. Her and I both find value in working on our craft and adding tools to our toolbox. I did not know it at the time, but after that weekend in Texas my mind-set on network marketing would never be the same.

It was at this event when I flipped on the windshield wipers and saw clearly. I can vividly remember my eyes being opened to the profession of network marketing. I knew the company I was with had great healthy products and that was why our family shared the benefits of our products and amazing company. After watching fifty speakers over three days, all of whom had different stories, personalities, tips, scripts, companies, products, and compensation plans, I started to fall in with the idea of the time and money freedom network marketing can offer. I realized that this is a business and legitimate profession—so much so that I told my wife, "Heaven forbid, if our current network marketing company ever goes bye-bye for whatever reason, I think we should research and join another company."

It was at this event when the wheels in my head were turning. I had found our path, and I understood that working harder meant more money and helping more people. After fifty speakers, I resonated with some and others not so much. As a whole I found them inspirational and educational. This was the exact weekend when my mind shifted to "this is a business and needs to be treated like a business." I realized I needed to place higher value on relationships, improve my speaking skills, develop tools for my team, and start taking massive action.

Fast forward several months, and with lots of effort and team building, my wife and my income had hit the amount needed for me to put in my two-week notice at my J-O-B and make the career switch to a full-time professional network marketer. The best part about this transition is that at the time I had a six-month-old baby boy I got to spend more time with and help out with. Our business structure is such a gift that we have not had to spend a single dime on daycare with our now two-year-old. Most families spend $14,000 a year on daycare per child to go make $35,000 a year before taxes.

I get excited knowing I can control my family's financial destiny—instead of a large corporation where I am crossing my fingers for a 4 percent raise. I urge you to push yourself and attend a couple three-day weekend network marketing events. They recharge you and give you new inspiration. One KEY component is to not just attend, but also get your team there! Many times

I have seen a great event and thought in my head who I should invite. Make a list of people you think would benefit from the event and call them with a personal invitation with the details. This is one way to create a positive team, by traveling to events and creating real bonding experiences.

Now that you are joining me in shifting your mind-set to clearly see this business as a credible profession, one of the best ways to stay on track in your business is by getting a great mentor. In the next section let's talk about why you need a good mechanic in your life!

CHAPTER 13

Mechanic

When you own a vehicle, a vital component is having a great mechanic—someone you can take your car in to for the normal tune-up, oil change, fluid flushes, etc. You also NEED this mechanic when something major goes wrong, like a blown transmission or a bad fuel pump, or even to install a new engine! What makes a good mechanic? I believe it is someone who gets under the hood, inspects the issues, and then delivers their honest recommendation without any hidden agendas. An excellent mechanic has the tools to fix the problems and get the vehicle on the road in no time! They say what the problem is even if the owner does not choose to hear it.

In network marketing, it is also important to have a good "mechanic" to help keep your car on the road. This person is called your mentor. I believe everyone needs a mentor in their network marketing journey—someone that can give you advice and shed some light on issues to get you back on the road.

The mentor can give you those slight tweaks in a tune-up to keep your business and mind-set running smoothly. Or during the times when you have blown your engine and are ready to quit this business, it can be your mentor that helps you do the repairs and get back on the road.

But remember, just like when your mechanic gives you advice on repairs and you don't choose to do them, when your mentor gives you advice, it still is your choice, your car, your time, your money. It is still up to you to take the advice and determine if you will do the repairs.

I would highly recommend finding a mentor that has already hit the rank or income you desire. They have done it before and, in my mind, have more credibility and knowledge to give you. I have been blessed to have my mentor, Marcella Vonn Harting. She gives it to you straight, and I respect her opinion. There have been many times when she has pushed me and gotten me out of my comfort zone. I listen and I trust that her thirty years of experience outweigh my opinion if I don't choose to do something. She is one of the hardest working professional network marketers I know. She has hit the highest rank and has the largest organization in her company, bringing in millions of dollars and over a million people.

Marcella is a mentor I admire, and when she says, "Luke, there is an event this Thursday in Orlando I think you should attend," I am booking my flight by lunch time and not responding with, "I can't afford it." The more you invest in yourself and your business, the larger returns you get. If I were to list the top ten themes she has pounded into my head, they would be the following:

1. This is a relationship-building business.

2. Leaders show up.

3. Be consistent over a long period of time.

4. It's the small things that make a difference.

5. Don't be afraid of rejection and don't take it

personally. (Marcella tells a great story about how when she was younger she worked at Burger King, and with every order she asked, "Would you like a soda and fries with that?" If the customer said no, she would not cry and go into therapy. She would simply ask the next customer, "Would you like a soda and fries with that?")

6. Integrity and ethics matter in this business.

7. Meet them where they are. This simply means if a member in your organization is not ready to do the business, don't force your dreams on them. If a member does not choose to host a class, don't make them. If a member chooses to work a booth at an expo, encourage them. Meet them where they are at. They may someday align with what you desire, but it will be much more powerful if they make the decision, not you. If your team member chooses to dive in and make a quick impact, you need to be prepared to ***strike while the iron's hot.*** This saying means act quickly with someone if they are ready and willing. Get a class on the books quickly, load them up with resources, and have them create a contact list.

8. It's not who you know; it's who they know.

9. No type of interaction beats face-to-face for building a relationship.

10. If money and time stop you from doing something you truly desire, money and time will always stop you.

Bonus 11. I could keep going, but personal growth is something Marcella echoes to anyone in any industry. Even you purchasing and reading this book is **personal growth**, so YOU are on the right path! (Typing out these eleven points, I can hear Marcella's voice in my head repeating them!)

In summary, for the mentor/mechanic, find someone who has accomplished what you desire to accomplish, and LISTEN to them.

We are now on the home stretch! The last chapter will give you something to think about each and every day.

CHAPTER 14

Hit the Roads

You are the only one that controls what type of leader you are going to be. You control who receives your treasured time, efforts, and resources. You control the amount of new people you get in front of to grow your network.

Right now, I'd like to challenge you: For the next thirty days, every time you get into your car and put your keys into the ignition (or hit the start button), take a quick moment and ask yourself the following questions:

What type of car am I going to be today?
What type of leader qualities will I show my team today?
What can I do today to strengthen a relationship?
Who deserves my precious time, efforts, and resources?

The roads are going to be bumpy, rocky, and icy on your network marketing road trip. You are going to drive into storms, get flat tires, and even get in an accident. There will be times where you are completely lost in the middle of nowhere with a dead cell phone feeling scared, alone, and tired. Just keep driving. The rain will stop, the sun will come out, the ice will melt, AAA will fix your tire, a mechanic will fix your car. Keep driving and you will soon recognize a familiar road and become lost no longer. Take action on income-producing activities, build many strong relationships, and invest in people that deserve it.

Rev up your business engine and hit the open roads!

Resources

www.LukeLangsweirdt.com

Here you can connect with Luke and Purchase Copies of the book. Bulk Discounts for your team are available.

www.DropOfKnowledge.com

Luke and his Wife Kortni's Blog

www.HighestPotentialAcademy.com

Subscribe to the news on the site for any upcoming event details

Made in the USA
Columbia, SC
28 July 2017